LETTERS

OF

SARAH DUCHESS OF MARLBOROUGH

AMS PRESS
NEW YORK

LETTERS

OF

SARAH DUCHESS OF MARLBOROUGH

NOW FIRST PUBLISHED FROM THE ORIGINAL

MANUSCRIPTS AT MADRESFIELD COURT

WITH AN INTRODUCTION

LONDON

JOHN MURRAY ALBEMARLE STREET

1875

Library of Congress Cataloging in Publication Data

Marlborough, Sarah (Jennings) Churchill, Duchess of,
    1660-1744.
    Letters of Sarah, Duchess of Marlborough.

    (Women of letters)
    1. Marlborough, Sarah (Jennings) Churchill,
Duchess of, 1660-1744. I. Series.
DA462.M4A25 1973   942.06'9'0924 [B]
ISBN 0-404-56766-5   77-37708

Reprinted from the edition of 1875, London
First AMS edition published, 1973
Manufactured in the United States of America

AMS PRESS, INC.
New York, N. Y.   10003

PREFACE.

N the Introduction to the following Letters of Sarah Duchess of Marlborough, it is attempted to be explained why their publication has been deemed desirable, as possessing an interest even at this time of day of no ordinary kind; whilst they fill up a void in Her Grace's published correspondence which has always been lamented by those who have had the curiosity to seek to acquaint themselves with the character and conduct of one who has figured so conspicuously at an important period of our country's history, and in close connection with perhaps as great, certainly as successful, a military hero as is to be met with in its annals, whether ancient or modern. One need but to call attention to Blenheim, and ask for even the slightest consideration of its origin and its object, to furnish sufficient illustration of this circumstance. That splendid palace of the Marlboroughs was a

Sovereign's grateful gift to the great Duke whose memorable achievements cast so brilliant a halo upon her reign. And not only was his distinguished Duchess an animating spirit in the victories he so signally accomplished, but for a long time she exerted great influence over the Queen herself, and Her Majesty's Government also, which powerfully affected the policy that was pursued with such triumphant results throughout one of the most momentous struggles with a foreign foe that have ever disturbed the serenity, or endangered the safety, of the British nation.

The volumes of Letters of Sarah Duchess of Marlborough already published, so far from having exhausted the subject, rather furnish a reason why these, which are now for the first time to meet the public eye, should supplement what has gone before, since they supply what has been regretted as an unfortunate deficiency, more particularly from their relating to a period of Queen Anne's reign, and a revolution in her Government, when it is of the deepest interest to learn what were the feelings and the opinions of those who, after having been such distinguished objects of Royal and of popular favour, were dismissed from the Court and the Government, and in consequence became for awhile exiles in a foreign land, where they were regarded, if not by the Queen, yet by Her Majesty's Ministers, as enemies to the true interests of the country and the cause they were once thought to have so faithfully served.

It may be thought strange, perhaps, that Letters of such public interest should so long have been left in obscurity. But the circumstances of their possession in private hands will amply account for this— circumstances, however, with which the public can have no concern. Not improbably, too, the fact of their being so completely private Letters may have had something to do with their having been hitherto withheld from publication. But at this distant day, any such consideration as that, it is felt, can no longer have any weight, more especially as they reveal no secrets which are of merely a personal kind, but principally such as are more or less of his- torical interest, and the publication of which can- not justly be said to violate any confidence, or perpetrate any other wrong. In that public point of view, in which it is but reasonable to regard them— for the whole subject of them more or less belongs to our national history—they may be fairly looked upon as completing a correspondence that was already before the public, and as therefore pleading, in some measure at least, their own justification for being thus rescued from oblivion.

It is true that some few of the Letters contain but petty details of very ordinary domestic matters :

still they are part and parcel of the Duchess's correspondence at a most interesting period of her own and her illustrious consort's public career; and on this ground it is thought desirable to include them with the rest. They all afford some indications of character which are not without interest in such a connection; and for this reason, if for no other, even trifles may be borne with which otherwise might be inexcusable.

It will be admitted, it is believed, that there is a plain-spokenness in these Letters, almost more strikingly displayed than in those that have been already published, and which furnishes some redeeming points in the Duchess of Marlborough's reputation. They appear, in short, to be on the whole, not only clever, but honest productions of Her Grace's facile pen. It is the remark of Sir Richard Steele, that 'there is no rule in the world to be made for writing letters, but that of being as near what you speak face to face as you can; which is so great a truth,' he adds, 'that I am of opinion writing has lost more mistresses than any one mistake in the whole legend of love.' The Duchess's Letters would certainly seem to verify that conclusion. Not, it is true, in any 'legend of love,' yet assuredly in a matter of Royal friendship and favour, Sarah Duchess of Marlborough's case, as revealed in her correspondence, does somewhat forcibly illustrate its truth, an epistolary 'mistake' having deprived Her Grace of the only opportunity that was presented to her of giving to her Royal Mistress, by word of mouth, as she knew so well how to do, such an explanation of her conduct as might have accomplished her complete vindication, and perhaps have had the happy effect of procuring the forgiveness, and recovering the affection, of 'the good Queen Anne.'

INTRODUCTION.

HE following Letters of Sarah Duchess of Marlborough form an interesting supplement to that published correspondence with which the reader of English History and Biography has long been familiar.

One of Her Grace's Biographers of a past age has remarked, that 'after the fall of the Whig Ministry in which the Duke took so powerful a part, during the remainder of the reign of Queen Anne very little of the correspondence of the Duchess of Marlborough is found;' and he accounts for this by the altered and adverse circumstances in which she was so precipitately placed. It was not, it must be remembered, the fall of the Whig Ministry only which made both these eminent personages to 'hide their diminished heads;' but it was the Duchess's utter forfeiture of the grace and favour of the Queen, her displacement from Her Majesty's affections by a

successful intriguer and hated rival, and her conse-
quent expulsion from Court in evident disgrace.

The circumstances under which all this arose
tended greatly to aggravate the Duchess's mortification. It was not without reason that she had
calculated upon exerting a life-long influence over
Queen Anne, who had taken every opportunity of
showing the warmest personal attachment towards
her. In their private correspondence, Her Majesty
was always spoken of as Mrs. Morley, and the Duke
and Duchess as Mr. and Mrs. Freeman. These dis-
guises, as we all know, were common in Court circles
at that day, being considered a prudent precaution
against the only too prevalent malice of party and
faction. The Duchess was in the habit of addressing
the Queen as 'My dear adored Mrs. Morley,' and
Her Majesty would speak of the Duchess's Letters,
in answering them, as 'so very kind, that, if it were
possible, you are dearer to me than ever you were;'
adding, 'I am so entirely yours, that if I might have
all the world given me, I could not be happy but in
your love.' The hasty rupture of an intimacy so
close, so ardent, as expressions such as these would
indicate it to have been, could not fail to be a terrible
blow to one in the Duchess's position, and Her Grace
evidently staggered under it for a long time afterwards. Not but that there had been temporary
quarrels on previous occasions; but there was then

no evil genius in the way to embitter their anger,
and to estrange their affection. No doubt, however,
the acrimonious altercations into which the Duchess
was ever and anon so unhappily betrayed laid the
foundation for that final breach which Mrs.
Masham, for her own and her friend Harley's
political and personal interests, eventually took
occasion to bring about.

There was thus a hand in the infliction of it
which added in no slight degree to its pain and
humiliation. No doubt it was a party as well as a
personal question that was involved in an intrigue
of which the Duchess became the victim; Mrs.
Masham being not only herself the Duchess's rival
in the Queen's regards, but also the tool of the
Duke's competitor for political ascendency.

Smollett the historian states that 'the Queen
began to show her attachment to the Tories by
mortifying the Duke of Marlborough.' But it was
evidently Mrs. Masham that was pulling the wires
all the while. Upon the death of the Earl of Essex
Her Majesty desired of the Duke that the regiment
which the Earl had commanded should be given to
Mrs. Masham's brother, Capt. Hill. The Duke
was thunder-struck. He remonstrated in the
strongest manner, insisting on the injurious prejudice
which the promotion of so young and inexperienced
an officer over older and abler men would produce

in the service. 'He expostulated, too, with his Sovereign,' we are told, 'on this extraordinary mark of partial regard to the brother of Mrs. Masham, which he could not help considering as a declaration against himself and his family, who had so much reason to complain of that lady's malice and ingratitude.' To this remonstrance, it is added, 'the Queen made no other reply but that he would do well to consult his friends. The Earl of Godolphin enforced his friend's arguments, though without effect ; and the Duke retired in disgust to Windsor.' It was now the Duchess's turn to confront the enemy that had so suddenly crossed what had hitherto been their 'path of glory.' She at once demanded an audience of Her Majesty, on the plea of vindicating her own character from certain aspersions which she alleged had been cast upon it. What ensued is thus described in the current history of the time :—' The Duchess hoped to work on the Queen's tenderness, and retrieve the influence she had lost. She protested, argued, wept, and supplicated ; but the Queen was too well pleased with her own deliverance from the tyranny of the other's friendship to incur such slavery for the future. All the humiliation of the Duchess served only to render herself the more contemptible. The Queen heard her without exhibiting the least sign of emotion, and all she would vouchsafe was a repetition of these words : " You desired no answer, and you shall have none," alluding to an expression in a letter she had received from the Duchess.' It is further recorded that, ' as an additional mortification to the Ministry, the office of Lord Chamberlain was transferred from the Duke of Kent to the Duke of Shrewsbury, who had lately voted with the Tories, and maintained an intimacy of correspondence with Mr. Harley. The interest of the Duke of Marlborough was not even sufficient to prevent the dismissal of his own son-in-law, the Earl of Sunderland, from the post of Secretary of State, in which he was succeeded by Lord Dartmouth.'

The usual ' honours' followed on the success of these intrigues. Mrs. Masham was styled Lady Masham, and Mr. Harley was created Earl of Oxford. But in a very short time some degree of retribution ensued. The Queen became exposed to severe trials by dissensions among her Ministers. ' Oxford and Bolingbroke,' we read, ' were competitors for power, and rivals in reputation and ability. The Treasurer's parts were deemed the more solid, the Secretary's more shining; but both Ministers were aspiring and ambitious. The first was bent on maintaining the first rank in the Administration, which he had possessed since the revolution in the Ministry ; the other disdained to act as a subaltern to the man whom he thought he

excelled in genius, and equalled in importance.
They began to form separate cabals, and to adopt
different principles. Bolingbroke insinuated himself
into the confidence of Lady Masham, to whom
Oxford had given some cause of disgust. By this
communication he gained ground in the good opinion
of his Sovereign, while the Treasurer lost it in the
same proportion. Thus she who had been the
author of his elevation was now used as the instru-
ment of his disgrace.' The Queen was painfully
affected by these contentions, and the cabals which
they originated ; so much so, indeed, that she retired
to Windsor disheartened and disgusted, and there
suffered under a severe and protracted illness, of
which they were mainly the cause, and certainly the
aggravation.

The only too evident vindictiveness of Lady
Masham towards the Duchess of Marlborough was
the less excusable from the circumstance of her being
Her Grace's relative, and as such under considerable
obligations to the Duke and Duchess of Marlborough. She was the daughter of Mr. Hill, a
merchant in London, by a sister of the Duchess's
grandfather. It is stated that he had twenty-two
children ; and his estate of £4,000 a-year had therefore at his decease to be divided into small portions,
of which Mrs. Masham's portion is said to have been
but £500. Harley was also a relation of the Hills.

The Duke of Marlborough did not escape the suspicion of having incited, in some degree, the party mischiefs which were disturbing the unanimity, if not also impairing the stability, of Her Majesty's Government, as well as affecting the health and happiness of the Queen herself. But it would not appear that there was any just ground for such suspicion, so far, at least, as the Duke himself was concerned, whatever there might be as respects the Duchess; though there was no proof, apparently, that even she, any more than the Duke, had interfered, or attempted to do so, for any such sinister purpose. That the Duke was angry with his wife for her violent conduct towards the Queen on several occasions was natural, and not undutiful; but his anger would seem to have soon passed away. In such a state of things, however, and finding his enemies becoming daily more and more implacable, he prudently decided to retire to the Continent. He left England alone, or only accompanied by a trusty personal attendant or two; but he was shortly followed by the Duchess, a reconciliation having evidently, without much difficulty, been effected. Nor is there anything in her Grace's numerous Letters from abroad to indicate the slightest want of connubial harmony, or cordiality.

The following Letters of the Duchess commence at a period shortly preceding the transactions just

referred to, continuing throughout the whole time of
their sojourn on the Continent, and extending to
three or four years beyond the Duke's decease, in
1722 : including the happier period of their restoration to Royal favour upon the accession of George
the First, and the restoration of the Duke to most of
the honours and emoluments of which he had been
deprived. The Duchess herself survived that date
more than two-and-twenty years—until the reign of
George the Second : thus prolonging her eventful
career through four successive reigns. Her death
is thus incidentally and somewhat heartlessly recorded by Smollett, in a note to Chapter V. of his
History (A.D. 1744)—the only record of it that he
has vouchsafed to give, notwithstanding the abundance of subject-matter she furnished for his pen :—
' Mr. Pope, the celebrated poet, died in the month of
June. In October the old Duchess of Marlborough
resigned her breath, in the 85th year of her age,
immensely rich, and very little regretted, either by
her own family or by the world in general.'

Her Grace, as it has already been mentioned, out-
lived the great Duke twenty-two years. But, with
all his greatness, and notwithstanding the lustre it
cast upon her own position, there is comparatively
little mention made of him in any of her letters
towards the close of his brilliant career, and scarcely
any allusion to his death in those written by her at

that time. The Duke's faculties, it would appear, had become greatly impaired, while the Duchess preserved her vigour of mind, and resoluteness of will, for many years afterwards. 'The Duke was interred,' it is recorded, 'in Westminster Abbey with such profusion of funeral pomp as evinced the pride and ostentation, much more than the taste and concern, of those who directed his obsequies.' Of the Duke, we believe, in his declining years, the remark of the poet was literally verified, whatever may have been the case with the Duchess :—

'From Marlborough's eyes the streams of dotage flow.'

Blenheim became the splendid palatial residence it now is during the life-time of the Duchess, though various domestic circumstances arose, into which we cannot enter here, to preclude the possibility of her ever enjoying it as a family residence. She took care, however, that it should not remain without some conspicuous memorial within its palatial pale of the Royal, as well as national, munificence to which the Marlboroughs owe so magnificent a possession. She erected a fine full-length statue of Queen Anne on a massive pedestal, bearing in its panels a long inscription from her own pen, gratefully testifying to the virtues, public and private, of Her Majesty—a memento that is highly creditable to the Duchess, as well as honourable to her Royal Mistress. She departed this life, ' full of years and honours,' as the chroniclers say, on the 18th of October, 1744.

The general subject of the Duchess's quarrel with Queen Anne has been so fully discussed in connection with Her Grace's published correspond-ence, that it would not be necessary to allude to it here, but for one element in it at least, that of the great uncongeniality of character which prevailed, having been too much overlooked. It is one that involves considerations which in our popular histories and biographies are generally so systematically ignored as often, if not to obscure the real bearing of certain historic transactions, yet certainly to exclude from them a degree of light which might, no doubt, have made them much better understood. It has never, perhaps, been particularly noted what a marked distinction there was between the Queen and the Duchess of Marlborough on the subject of religion and the Church. It is quite probable, of course, that during the period of their closest and most affectionate intimacy Queen Anne had not yet taken the warm interest in such matters that she subsequently felt. But at any rate there is reason to believe that Her Majesty's gradual discovery not merely of the Duchess's indifference to religion, but of her hostility to the Church, in those higher aspects, at least, in which the Queen had come to regard it, had no little to do, personally and privately, not only in estranging Her Majesty's affections, but also in forfeiting her respect. But any direct evidence of this, in these Letters, is merely, it must be confessed, of a negative kind. Whenever the Duchess has occasion to allude to the subject, it is only, in substance, to reiterate that she is ' a Protestant,' and this in scarcely any other sense than that of an anti-Romanist. She seldom, if ever, gives expression, even in immediate connection with the subject, to any religious thought, or any Church sentiment; nor was there anything, whether in her private or public character or career, that indicated a serious concern for either the one or the other. She has, however, elsewhere put on record her idea of and her feeling toward the Church in terms which, though brief and cursory, are yet sufficiently significant. It occurs in a ' Letter to Lord ——,' entitled ' An Account of the Conduct of the Duchess of Marlborough from her first coming to Court to the year 1710,' published in London in 1742, in which she says, alluding to Queen Anne, 'For my own part I had not the same prepossessions [for the Church]. The word CHURCH had never any charm for *me*, in the mouths of those who made the most noise with it; for I could not perceive that they gave any other distinguishing proof of their regard for the *thing* than a frequent use of the *word*, like a spell to enchant weak minds;

and a persecuting zeal against Dissenters, and against those real friends of the Church who would not admit that persecution was agreeable to its doctrine.' Such was the popular liberal cant of that day, as it is indeed of our own time ; and puritanism and worldliness are, and ever have been, at one upon it. It strikingly shows in the case before us what an element of discord, and of animosity, there was in the Duchess's heart and mind as respects Queen Anne, notwithstanding, for a while, their seeming attachment to each other. Another allusion is made to this subject in the published 'Account of her Conduct,' etc., just referred to. She is speaking of another Letter to some great personage that she had prepared for publication, the object of which, she says, is 'to give an account of my conduct with respect to parties, and of the successful artifice of Mr. Harley and Mrs. Masham, in taking advantage of the Queen's passion for what she called the Church, to undermine me in her affections.' She belonged too, it must be remembered, to a party which then, as it does still, seldom hesitated to range itself in hostility to the Church, and which included in its ranks, as it continues to do, most of those who sought, either directly or indirectly, the Church's overthrow—many of them, in fact, the overthrow of religion itself.

Now Queen Anne, we repeat, was in all those

respects a very different character from Sarah Duchess of Marlborough. Even Smollett, who had but little sympathy with such Royal virtues, has yet been constrained to acknowledge, and has almost affected to appreciate them, in the case of Queen Anne. 'She was zealously attached,' he declares, 'to the Church of England from conviction rather than from prepossession, unaffectedly pious, just, charitable, and compassionate,'—Christian graces that were anything but conspicuous in the Duchess of Marlborough. 'She felt,' the same historian continues, 'a mother's fondness for her people, by whom she was universally beloved with a warmth of affection which even the prejudice of party could not abate. In a word,' he adds, 'if she was not the greatest, she was certainly one of the best and most unblemished sovereigns that ever sat upon the throne of England, and well deserved the expressive, though simple epithet of " The Good Queen Anne."' That Her Majesty's being a devout Christian and earnest-minded Churchwoman had every thing to do with what constituted her 'one of the best and most unblemished of sovereigns that ever sat upon the throne of England' will not, for a moment, we think, be disputed by anyone capable of forming an opinion upon the question. The Duchess herself, indeed, has expressed a decided opinion of the Queen's unaffected piety and equity, emphatically declaring of Her Majesty, in one of her published letters, 'She was religious without affectation, and certainly meant to do everything that was just.' True, on another occasion, she attributes Her Majesty's Church polity, if not also her religious feelings, to a lower motive, when she states that 'the Queen was very much *bigoted* to the Tories or Church party, as they affected to call themselves, thereby insinuating that the Whigs were all Dissenters, and enemies thereto'—that is to the Church. But this idea was altogether of a political character. And there can be little doubt that the Duchess's own real sentiments on the subject, as one of public concern, were altogether of such a character.

An able and impartial Church historian of our own day, remarking upon the state of things ecclesiastical at the period of Queen Anne's accession, appositely says—' It was at this time that the terms High Church and Low Church first began to be used, originally in the House of Commons. The latter name was given to those who sided with Government in opposing the Church and favouring Dissenters, whilst the former title designated the opposite party. Most of the Bishops in this (William's) reign being appointed by Government influence, naturally belonged to the Low Church section.'[1] There can be no feeling of surprise, therefore, when he goes on to say, that ' Queen

---

[1] Blunt's ' Key to Church History.'

Anne, as a member of the exiled Stuart family, and professedly a firm Churchwoman, was gladly welcomed by many to whom the late Sovereign had been very unacceptable.' It was that very Government, let it be borne in mind, to which the House of Marlborough belonged ; and it was whilst such a policy was being pursued that the then all-powerful Duchess succeeded in ingratiating herself with the new Sovereign. Queen Anne, however, saw through it all in due time, and then came the revulsion, the Duchess's mortifications under which are so constantly, though often complacently, exhibited in the following correspondence. Alluding to the period of the Queen's accession, the historian we have just quoted further observes—' The Court and Government was now given up to Anti-Church influence, through the ascendency of the Marlborough faction.' This is pointed enough. But it is strictly true ; and none, one may be sure, had greater weight in the ' Marlborough faction' than the Marlboroughs themselves ; as no one, it may well be believed, was more potent, or had greater opportunities, for mischief, being, as she was, for only too long a period in the ascendant over the Queen herself, than Sarah Duchess, whose are the Letters which follow.

The sudden and violent estrangement that arose is much more clearly explained in connection with these circumstances than it could otherwise be ; for the attachment that for some time subsisted, as we have already shown, was evidently one of no ordinary character. According to the Duchess's own statement of their intimacy—which has been already incidentally alluded to, and there is no reason to doubt its correctness—the Queen was habitually demonstrating her love and regard for her favourite. 'It was this turn of mind,' Her Grace stated, 'which made her one day propose to me that whenever I should happen to be absent from her, we might in all our letters write ourselves by feigned names, such as would import nothing of distinction of rank between us. Morley and Freeman were the names her fancy hit upon; and she left me to choose by which I should be called. My frank, open temper naturally led me to pitch upon Freeman, and so the Princess took the other; and from this time Mrs. Morley and Mrs. Freeman began to converse as equals.' Not improbably one reason for Anne proposing this course of correspondence might be a fear lest her sister, Queen Mary, should on any occasion intercept their letters. For Her Majesty had a strong aversion to the Duchess, and did all in her power to set Anne against her, until, at length, on the plea that the Duke was dismissed by King William from all his appointments, and in disgrace at Court, she insisted on the Princess dismissing the Duchess also, and excluding her too altogether from the

Court. Anne, however, warded off this blow as long as she could, and their correspondence as Mrs. Morley and Mrs. Freeman would seem to have continued, and to have shown more and more the strong attachment of the Princess. The settlement by Anne of £2,000 a-year on the Duchess was one among many instances of the ardency of that attachment. And we learn, with respect to this, that some little delay having arisen in the payment of it by her Treasurer, Anne wrote to the Duchess thus :—' 'Tis long since I mentioned this thing to dear Mrs. Freeman. She has all the reason in the world to believe I did not mean what I said, or that I have changed my mind, which are both so ill qualities that I cannot bear you should have cause to think your faithful Morley is capable of being guilty of either.' An attachment like this, then, would not be rudely and ruthlessly severed without some extraordinary cause ; and such a cause may not unreasonably, under all the circumstances, be found in that disagreement which Anne had come to regard as involving vital principles, religious and political— their disagreement, namely, on the grave questions of religion and the Church.

It may be thought, perhaps, that these remarks would have been more appropriate in an Introduction to a more general collection of the Duchess of Marlborough's published correspondence than to one so limited, and merely supplemental, as the present is. But they are not altogether out of place even here; and they will be excused, it is hoped, if only on the ground that they are such as have probably never been so pointedly made before. That the Duchess was deeply mortified, not to say violently angered, by the Queen's conduct towards her, it is impossible to doubt; yet it will be seen that she but slightly displays her mortification, or her anger, in the fcllowing letters, although they were written, many of them, almost immediately after the painful occurrences which have here been referred to.

In nothing is Queen Anne's partiality for the Duchess, ere the rupture arose, more strikingly evinced than in Her Majesty's lavish bestowal of permanent pecuniary grants upon Her Grace, in addition to the accumulating payments which at one period swelled the Duke's own income to nearly £55,000 a-year. The following is a published statement of the Duchess's regular emoluments :—As Keeper of the Great and Home Parks, £1,500; as Mistress of the Robes, £1,500; as Keeper of the Privy Purse, £1,500; as Groom of the Stole, £3,000; together with a pension out of the Privy Purse of £2,000—total annual income of Her Grace £9,500. And according to the Duchess's account, these munificent amounts were not only

most deliberately arranged, but most resolutely enforced, by the Queen herself. It must, therefore,
have been something far higher than any political
or personal prejudice which could cause so sudden
and violent a change of feeling as Anne's subsequent
estrangement from the Duchess, and apparent an-
tipathy to her, so remarkably exhibited; and that
something, we repeat, is only to be discovered in the
intense consciousness of the Queen that upon a subject which, above all others, Her Majesty had come
to regard as of vital moment to the prosperity of
her kingdom, her quondam favourite, and once too
frequent flatterer, was most grievously at fault.

The item of £2,000 a-year from the Privy Purse
having been called in question, the Duchess, it is on
record, inserted the following statement in her accounts :—' After the Princess came to the Crown she
was pleased to write to me to take £2,000 a-year
out of the Privy Purse, and make no words of it,
and lay it up to do something with; because, she
added, she had not power to do as others had done
before her, to reward faithful services,—that I might
own it or conceal it as I liked best, for she did not
care who knew what she gave to one she could
never reward enough.' We also have it attested by
the Duchess herself how generous Anne was in her
provision for the future as well as for the present.
' The Queen,' Her Grace states, ' never forgot her

promises of providing for all my children, which she fully performed.' When their connection became broken off, a demand would appear to have been made, from a hostile quarter, to have the Duchess's accounts examined ; and the following is Her Grace's own version of the result :—' Her Majesty, after keeping my accounts a sufficient time to have them carefully examined (I suppose by Mr. Harley), re-turned them to me signed in this manner :—" *Feb.* 1, $17\frac{10}{11}$. *I have examined these accounts, and allow them. Anne R.*" ' Coldly formal though this acknowledg-ment is, even as a mere voucher, it is yet a suffi-cient justification of the Duchess as regards the question at issue ; while it certainly involves con-siderations which go far to strengthen the argument we have already adduced.

But this correspondence, it will be observed, is by no means confined to public affairs. Much of it has reference to private and personal matters, and even domestic details. Some of it may on this ac-count appear trivial and insignificant, and under ordinary circumstances it would probably deserve to be so regarded. But Sarah Duchess of Marl-borough was an extraordinary character, and her name has an historic renown which gives an interest, more or less, to everything connected with her. Besides, there prevails in educated English society a not altogether unreasonable curiosity to know all that can be learned of the home-life of its country's historic personages, we might almost say of the inner life, which so generally affords the truest insight into the real character of such personages, and so often gives the clew to hidden motives. It is perhaps an advantage that these Letters do deal so largely with the Duchess's private and personal concerns and those of her illustrious husband, since the correspondence which has already met the public eye is mainly, if not altogether, devoted to affairs of State: though, at the same time, many of these Letters are by no means devoid of interest in that respect. It is not often that the broils and bitternesses of political life, or the tainted atmosphere of courts, can conduce to the enjoyment of domestic happiness and repose. The idea of the poet, it is to be feared, is not frequently realised, that

> ' At home the hateful names of parties cease,
> And factious souls are weary'd into peace.'

But it is interesting to know whether this is ever the case or not in the homes of such as have figured so prominently, and often amid so much greatness and grandeur, as did Sarah Duchess of Marlborough ; and these Letters, therefore, are for that, among other reasons, even in their most private and personal details, calculated to afford both entertainment and instruction.

The Duchess's system of orthography, which is

preserved as found to prevail throughout the whole correspondence, however vulgar and illiterate it may now appear, was that which in her day and generation was generally in vogue in the highest classes of English society. But it is not, it will be perceived, a strictly uniform system. It extended, too, it will be seen, to the names of persons as well as things. The name of the person to whom most of the following Letters are addressed, which was also her own maiden name, is spelled in two or three different ways. In the later years of her active life there is a slight improvement in Her Grace's spelling ; and this may not improbably have been owing to the greater attention that had come to be paid to orthography in the education of the rising generation. The circumstance of one of her grandchildren—called to act as the Duchess's amanuensis on a certain emergency—spelling what was written with almost faultless propriety, certainly encourages, if it does not indicate, this idea. Dean Swift has pointed out as ' a cause which hath maimed our language, a foolish notion that we ought to spell exactly as we speak ;' facetiously though forcibly adding that, ' since in London they clip their words after one manner about the Court, another in the City, and a third in the Suburbs, all this reduced to writing must entirely confound orthography.' But in the case before us this would scarcely account for the bad

spelling that is to be complained of. The fact is,
that correct spelling was seldom or never, we
believe, acquired at school in the Duchess's
youthful days, and therefore seldom or never
adopted ; and this owing to the circumstance, not
improbably, of orthography not having yet become
a settled and determinate thing in the English language.

In other published correspondence of Sarah
Duchess of Marlborough, the device of cyphers is
shown to have been systematically used. But in
these Letters it has not been so adopted. In one of
them, however, a set of cyphers is given, but without
any instructions as to their employment ; although
allusion is occasionally made to the insecurity of
correspondence by post, more especially from abroad,
and in cases where the parties corresponding were
suspected to be disaffected towards the existing Ministry. The cyphers, or numerals, here referred to
were twenty-five in number, and represented many
of the leading public characters of the day, including
the Queen, and the Duke and Duchess of Marlborough themselves. It is remarked in one of the
editions of the Marlborough Correspondence that has
been some time published, that 'from the 16th to
the end of the 18th century public men used
cyphers in their correspondence, for it was not till a
comparatively late period that the post was a safe

conveyance. About the time of which we are now writing,' it is added, ''numbers were generally used for this purpose, to which sometimes were given the signification of letters, and at others of words. In the correspondence of the Duchess of Marlborough and Lord Godolphin with the Duke of Marlborough, the only cyphers used are a series of numerals which stood for names of people and countries, and some party names, etc., which to those unacquainted with their signification were a sufficient disguise to the meaning.' The numerals attached to one of the following Letters were probably the same as those referred to in this quotation. Strange, however, that there should be no employment of them, with a single exception, in a correspondence so much of which was from abroad, and in which the risk of safety and security by the post is repeatedly alluded to. But it will be observed that the Duchess is somewhat cautious in her allusions to the existing Administration, and is especially reticent and reserved in any mention of Her Majesty the Queen.

Not these Letters only, but all the published correspondence of Sarah Duchess of Marlborough, show her Grace to have had 'the pen of a ready writer'—to have been, in fact, a facile and an accomplished correspondent: wonderfully so, indeed, for a lady of that period—although it is quite true she was by no means an ordinary character, even in those

higher circles in which she so conspicuously and for
a long time so brilliantly shone.   The great interest
of her correspondence arises, of course, from the ex-
alted position which she occupied, and the peculiar
opportunities she enjoyed of becoming acquainted
with the most private. affairs of the Court, and often
the most critical situations of the Government.   But
independently of such attractions as these, whether
in their political or personal aspect, the Letters are
interesting and valuable as models of a good epistolary style.   Congreve, in one of his imitations of
Ovid, remarks—

> ' Be sure, avoid set-phrases when you write,
> The usual way of speech is more polite.'

Sarah Duchess of Marlborough was one who had
evidently profited by this injunction.   Montaigne,
alluding to the epistolary conventionalities of his
own time and country, says—' The letters of this
age consist more in foldings and fine prefaces than
matter ; where I had rather write two letters than
close and fold up one, and always assign that employment to some other ; as also when the business
of my letter is despatched, I would with all my heart
transfer it to another hand, to add those long
harangues, offers, and prayers we place at the
bottom, and should be glad that some new custom
should discharge us from that unnecessary trouble ;
as also superscribing them with a long ribble-row of

qualities and titles, which, for fear of mistakes, I have several times given over writing, especially to men of the long-robe.' The Duchess of Marlborough, in her correspondence, has acted very much in the spirit of such remonstrances as these. Save when displeased or disturbed, she was a remarkably courteous writer : somewhat too lavish of compliment, and over fond of flattery sometimes ; but all that belonged to the age, and was encouraged by circumstances. Its indulgence rarely interfered, however, with the real and generally substantial object of her communications ; and at no time would she appear to have sacrificed the *suaviter in modo* for the *fortiter in re.*

Making all due allowance for the suspicion of partiality, in being a witness in her own cause, it would not seem unreasonable to conclude, after an unprejudiced perusal of these Letters, that, with all her faults, Sarah Duchess of Marlborough was not deserving of much of the obloquy that was so persistently cast upon her, not only during her lifetime, but for a long while afterwards. Political animosity and party spirit had of course much to do with the vituperative attacks that were made upon her. One who evidently cherished a rancorous hatred of her was Harley, Earl of Oxford ; though his letter to Her Grace, which will be found in the following correspondence, and which will now for the first time, we believe, meet the public eye, conveys an emphatic assurance of Harley's disbelief of many of the charges made against her. Whether or not Harley was sincere, may no doubt admit of dispute; for sincerity was a rare virtue with public men of that day, and all the fashionable conventionalities, alike of political and social life, were as hollow as the wind. Among the more witty, but not the less malicious, of the Duchess's assailants was Pope, the poet; and it is a significant circumstance that one of the severest satires on Her Grace obtained posthumous publicity through her bitter enemy, Harley. We allude to the poem of 'Atossa, a Satire on Woman,' first published, we believe, in the 'Harleian Miscellany,'—a collection of unpublished manuscripts and other papers, tracts, etc., found in his library after his decease. It is, in the 'Miscellany,' entitled, 'The Character of a certain great Duchess, deceased; by a certain great Poet, lately deceased.' But it sadly overshoots the mark; and as well as being characterised by malevolence, it is full of misrepresentations. For instance, it says :—

> 'For sixty years this world has been her trade,
> The wisest fool that time has ever made;
> From loveless youth to unrespected age,
> No passion gratified except her rage.'

Now here, within four lines, there are as many calumnies. (1) The world was *not* her trade in any such special sense as Pope implies—not more so, we dare say, than it was his own, although after another fashion. (2) And certainly she was no fool, wise or otherwise. (3) Neither was she 'loveless' in her youth ; on the contrary, she was one of the most lovely women of the day, and from all reliable accounts, at that time as lovable as she was lovely ; and loving, it was believed, very sincerely Colonel Churchill, whom she married in preference to other and richer suitors. (4) Whilst as to gratifying, as years advanced, no other passion than her rage, the following Letters contain a good deal that decidedly contradicts it also. There is a couplet that comes after the above quotation which further displays the unscrupulousness of the poet, namely :—

> 'But what are these to great Atossa's mind,
>   Scarce once herself, by turns all womankind ? '

This correspondence certainly shows no such in-consistency, no such versatility of character. But the truth was, we repeat, that Pope, for some reason or other, had a deadly spite against her, a fact which the following extract sufficiently corroborates :—

> 'Atossa, cursed with every granted prayer,
>   Childless with all her children, wants an heir.
>   To heirs unknown descends th' augmented store,
>   Or wanders, Heaven-directed, to the poor.'

This, to say the least of it, as every one acquainted

with the Duchess's case must admit, is a great exaggeration, and a most malicious insinuation. Dr. Johnson was evidently very much of our opinion when, in his Life of Pope, in the ' British Poets,' he declared—' The time soon came in which it was safe to display the Duchess of Marlborough under the name of *Atossa*; and her character was inserted with no great honour to the writer's gratitude.'

The mention of Congreve and Montaigne has a personal interest in connection with our subject— more especially as regards Congreve, to whom, it will be remembered, there is a conspicuous monument in Westminster Abbey, which records its having been erected by Henrietta, Duchess of Marlborough, who is said to have entertained a warm regard for the poet, and to whom, in preference to claims of kindred or to humbler friendships, he left the bulk of his fortune. Henrietta was the daughter of Sarah Duchess of Marlborough, and succeeded to the title under a special Act of Parliament. She died in 1733, eleven years after the death of her father, and eleven years before the death of her mother. Montaigne belonged to a previous age— nearly two centuries before. But he was one for whose works Sarah Duchess of Marlborough is understood to have had a great admiration—his Essays in particular—though she was not familiar with them in their native language. The Duchess

would not seem, however, to have invariably profited by such preceptors.

The Mr. Jennens, or Jennings, to whom the
greater portion of the following Letters were written,
was a relative of the Duchess's, and a London
lawyer of eminence, and of substance.   Sarah
Duchess of Marlborough was the daughter of
Richard Jennens, or Jennings, Esq., of Sandridge,
in Hertfordshire, through whom the relationship
existed.   One of the family, Colonel Robert Jennens,
was A. D. C. to King William the Third; and his
wife was Anne Guidott, sister, we believe, of the
Mr. Guidott whose name occurs so frequently in
the following correspondence.   The Jennenses from
whom the Duchess was descended were an old and
good family in Hertfordshire; and Her Grace of
Marlborough was co-heiress with her sister, the
Duchess of Tyrconnel, and enjoyed her large
portion of the estates until her death.   Being
extremely handsome and attractive, and introduced
at Court very young, as a Lady of the Bedchamber
to Anne, Princess of Denmark, she soon established
her reputation as one of the 'Court Beauties' of
the day.

Letters

OF THE

Duchess of MARLBOROUGH.

SECTION FIRST.

HE following Letters of Sarah Duchess of Marlborough are divided into Three Sections. The first embraces the period immediately preceding her quarrel with Queen Anne, and the defeat and disgrace of the Whig Ministry, of which the Duke and Duchess were the life and soul. The second comprises the period of their exile, which arose from their being in disgrace at Court, and objects of animosity and annoyance with the Government. And the third includes the period subsequent to their return home, and their restoration to royal favour after the death of Queen Anne and the accession of George I. The year, it will be observed, but seldom forms part of the date; but it is given on conjecture, in several instances, by the Editor. The omission is, generally speaking, not very material; though it would certainly have been more satisfactory to have had the exact year. Along with the last letter in Section First, relating to the Duchess's expulsion from Court, there is given a letter from Mr. Harley which very considerably exonerates her Grace, and is altogether most favourable to her case.

To Mr. Jennens.

Jan. the 8th, *London.*

I have thought of writing to you twenty Times since you left London, but having Nothing to say that was of any Service to you, I have myself been prevented with the miserable hurrys that you have seen in this Place, and concluded that an insignificant Letter would be no Loss to you, but now I must give you a thousand Thanks for your kind Letter to me, though it gives me a great deal of Pain, and I long mightyly to hear from you again, and to know that your dear Son continues in the same good Way you thought him when you wrote to me. I wish with all my Soul that he had had that cruell Disease when I could have assisted dear Mrs. *Jennens* in looking after him, which I am sure I would have done with more Care and Tendernesse than anybody in the World except herself. I began this Year with being lucky at Play, having won at Dise with the King 568 Guineas, which makes me hope I shall not bee un-lucky to you in our Tickitts, but I will say no more of such Things till I know your Mind is quit at ease, which I hope you will have the Goodnesse to tell me very soon.

No. 2.

To Mr. Jennens.

Jan. the 11th, *Tuesday.*

I beg you to write me two Lines to put me out of Pain for your dear Son, for I am really very impatient to hear of him, which I have not don since your Letter that gave the first Account of his having the Small Pox, and I have sent to your Hous, and they knew Nothing. God Almighty preserve him to you. We have wone 70 Pounds in the Lottery, that I have look'd over Yesterday, but nothing of that Kind is worth writing upon.

No. 3.

To Mr. Jennens.

Saturday.

I give you a thousand Thanks for the Favour of yours of the 11th January, which relieved me of a great Deal of Pain ; for I had sent to your Son's and could learn Nothing but that your Son was very full of that dreadfull Disease, and I apprehended very much that some sad Turn had happend, though you were so easy when you first wrote to me upon it. I rejoyce with you and dear Mrs. *Jennens* from the Bottom of my Heart for this great Deliverance, and I hope now it is all over, she will take as much Care of herself as she did of her dear Son, who I wish may never give her a Minet's Pain again, but study to return his whole Life, in a better Manner than mere Children do, the great Care and Tendernesse that I am sure she has, and will ever have, for him. Tho' you are so indifferent as to our Lottery, I can't help telling you that I had Ten Prizes in about 30 of our Tickets, but they were all paltery Things, two of 50 Pounds, and the other eight 20 each. I thank you for your kind Care of my small Affairs. I shall observe your Directions if the Servant comes to me, and am as I ought to be most faithfully yours.

No. 4.

To Mrs. Jennens.

Windsor Castle, Aprill the 8th.

I was very sorry to leave London, Madam, without waiting upon you, which I intended very often, and to have beg'd the Favour of you and Mr. *Jenyns* to have come to me, but it is impossible for you to imagin the Hurry I am in when I am at St. James's, and the Court in Town, and it would be ridiculous to discribe it, but I hope before the Sumer is gon to have an Opertunity of seeing you, and in the mean time I was incouraged by something Mr. *Jenyns* said to beg a Favour of you, that you would sometimes call upon the Woman that is working my Bed with Poynt, when you goe that way, and it is no great Trouble to you, for without your Advise I doubt she will never finish it like that which Mrs. *Reeves* begun, and with your Assistance I might yet hope to see it a very fine Thing. If I did not believe you very good I should never have taken such a Liberty as to have ask'd you such a Favour, which I should be glad to return if it were possible for me to bee of any Use to you, being very sincerely, dear Mrs. *Jenyns*, your most obedient and most humble Servant,

S. MARLBOROUGH.

My humble Services to Mr. *Jenyns*. I hope your pretty Son is well.

No. 5.

To Mrs. Jennens.

Wednesday Morning.

I trouble dear Mrs. *Jennens* with this to let her know that wee have found Diamonds to button back the *Monto* and *Dye's* coat, so that all the Diamonds you have may be used upon the Sleeves if you please. Before I send to a third to play at Ombra to-night, I desire to know if Mr. *Jennens* likes to play; but as I believe Lady *Burlingham* can't come, Lady *Pembroke* will play but Half-crowns. I won't desire you to dine here if it is uneasy, but we never goe to Dinner till half-an-hour after Two; all I can say is that you will both be very wellcome, and I have wonderfull good Ale.

No. 6.

To Mrs. Jennens.

I give you many Thanks, dear Mrs. *Jenens*, for all your Goodnesse to me, which sometimes I fear makes me too troublesome. This little Money is for *Dye's* Affair, and I beg of you to send me those Bills again, if it is not quite as well as containing Money. The reason I send them so is that all that the Duke of *Marlborough* pays is done in this manner.

I am ever yours.

Tuesday Night—too late to send. I wish I may hear Mr. *Jennens* had a good Night at the return of his Messenger.

To Mrs. *Jennens.*

Whatever has been the Cause of Mr. *Jennens's* Illnesse ? I hope it is over, and that it is not of a dangerous Sort. If you care to have any of my beloved Sir *W. Rawleigh's* Cordial, I will send you some very good of Doctor *Gibson's* making.

I can find but these 34 Diamonds upon the Knott. I hope there is all you put. If I did not mistake you two on the Bottom were mine, which are on still. Send me Word if you have all you should have.

Dear Mrs. *Jennens*, I am sorry for the Fright you have been in.

Day.

To Mr. *Jennens.*

Feb. the 16th, O. S.

I write to you by a Man that brought Writings to sign in great Hast, and could not answer all you said in yours of the 2nd of this Month ; and I am sure I can never sufficiently thank you for all the Pains you take in our Affairs, and you must be contented with having Vertue, which the Stoicks say is its own Reward. What you say of the Rules to be given at *Woodstock* is intirely right ; and in a proper Time I love to bee rid of Everybody I know to be a Rogue, and take my Chance for the next. The D. of *M.* wrote lately to this Effect, that hee would have

any Estate bought that his Friends thought a good
Purchase, but that it was natural for him to prefer
any Purchase in *Oxfordshire* or *Hertfordshire* before
any other if they were equally good Bargains ; and
I think next to those two Countys *Bedfordshire* is
the best, for 'tis between his Estate at St. *Alban's*
and that of *Holdenby* that you seeme so well satisfyd
with.   Thirty Pounds a-Year was my Agreement
for his Allowance ; I mean Mr. *Montjo.* I can't
remember to what Time hee was paid, but in the
Account which I gave you of that Estate I remember I write what was necessary for you to know, as
perticularly that the Person had Mony charged in
an Account past that was not due but in one that
was not then come in.   I shall not trouble you with
much more upon *Cox's* Subject, having done so so
fully allready, only this, that Nothing was ever so
impudent as his last Intention of paying his own
Rents to the D. of *Marl.*, that were stated by *Hodges*
first and *C. Mydd.* at the Time that the D. of *Marl.*
was in the Hous, and after I had him in Town when
the D. of *Marl.* was gon out of *England*, it was all
looked over again by the Goldsmith by St. *Clement's*
Church.   *Cox* and *Middleton* sent for to *London*
again, and at that Time not the least Pretence of
having paid any of his Arrear, but some Dispute
about a very small Thing between *Cox* and *Myddleton* of about Ten Pounds, which *Cox* said hee had
paid *Mydleton*, and hee had not charged it in his
Account, but hee said hee would doe it.   This is
of no Consequence but to shew the Villany of *Cox.*

I am now come to yours of the 8th, in which, as
well as in many others, you shew you have taken
more Pains about Ld. *Marlborough's* Affairs than
ever hee did himself, notwithstanding the Passion
Mr. Examiner *Lee* says hee has for Mony. As to
the Garden Account, I believe it is much the same
for many Yeares ; but that which I observed and did
not much admire was in Accounts that I believe
are so old that you never saw them. I find that
when the D. of *Marl.* lived all were allways in the
Country. When hee was out of Favour with King
William, and some Time afterwards, I cast up ten
Yeares' Accounts at St. *Alban's*, and found the Garden Expense was, one Yeare with an other, a hundred
and sixty Pounds a Yeare, and I am sure then they
did not require so much Cost, at least, as now that
many Things might be saved, and no doubt are
saved, that wee can't be sensible of. As for the
Pigeon Hous, if that bee a great Expense, 'tis ridiculous for People that never live there ; and I remember when I was at *London* the Pigeons hee
sometimes sent were not good, and I was answered
when I found Fault that they had not so much
Feeding as they ought to have. Pray doe what you
please in that Matter, or in any Thing else. I am
apt to think they cover some Abuses in the Repairs
by making use of the Duke of *Marl.'s* Name without any Authority for doing so, for hee assures me
that hee gave no Directions for any Repairs, and
hee adds that hee was asked to order Things a

hundred Times by *C. M.* and Mr. *Carter*, but allways refus'd it, for hee says that all the Tenants are
oblidged to do it themselves by their Leases, and
that he is sure, if he had comply'd with what
was desir'd, it would have cost him a very great
Sum of Money, and the Farmes would have been
such as they are now; and after the D. of *Marl.*
was gone out of *England*, upon finding that severall
Bills in the Accounts, and charged without any
Order, or anybody's signing the Bills, I told *C. M.,*
nay, I put in the written Orders that hee had from
me, that for the Time to come there should not bee
a Shilling layd out upon any such Account but what
you directed; so that he calls a Bill of £62 0s. 11*d.,*
delivered to the D. of *Marl.,* I don't know the
Meaning of, nor of the Repaires at *Sandridge*, unless
you ordered it; and if you look over the very last
Account of *C. Mydd.* you will find, I believe, as well
as Mr. *Cox*, Money paid upon that Head without
any Manner of Satisfaction given to the D. of *M.*
or to me why it was paid. I never knew anything
of Mr. *Carter* but that hee was honest, but 'tis out
of his Businesse to hinder the Trade from going on
that hee professes and lives by, and it is unpardon-
able to say I presume to order him to do anything,
after what had been said, that you don't approve of.
I allways expected such an Account as you give of
the *Oxfordshire* Estates, which would be to no Purpose to tell me, because I know Nothing perticular
of anything there but Mr. *R.*; but as to any Ques-

tions you have to ask pray don't spair me when you
are at Leisure yourself, for 'tis quit new to make
Excuses for troubling me in my own Businesse, besides that I have not much to doe here; and yet
I have write this so fast I think 'tis hardly possible
for you to read it. I reckon now, very soon, you
will bee busy with Parliament. I don't much like
a Thing I heard of the Gentleman that *R.* begins
not to think well of, that hee professes much to bee
for the Protestant Succession, but is not att all persuaded there is any Danger of the P. of *W.*, and
that I think is the exact Stile of Sir *Ro.*, that hee
will come into any Thing for the Security of the
Protestant Suc.; but the Whigs must begin that.
Now, according to my plain simple Way of Thinking,
I apprehend this to bee some Trick; for if a great
Lady who is now so well in her Health will bee
angry that any Thing should bee don to secure that,
what is the Difference between those Men that
begin it, or those that joyn in the doing it? But
why should one imagin that a Person who con-
siderd Religion before her Father should not like
to take Care of that Poynt in case we should be so
unfortunate as to loose her? Has not the *Q.* her
Sister confessed that she should live in *England,*
tho she was the next Heir, with so much Virtue as
made it very dangerous?

No. 9.

To Mrs. Jennens.

Friday, nine in the Morning.

I hear you are to be of our Party to-day, dear Mrs. *Jennens*. I don't know how soon it is necessary for us to sett out to be at *Kensington* a little before Three, and the Duke of *Marlborough* is but such a weak, and I am not certain at what Houre it will be easy for him to goe; but if you and Mr. *Jennens* will be so good as to goe with us upon the Conditions that I whisperd in your Eare, we will call you at the Hour you shall send Word is the latest wee must come, and as much sooner as it happens to bee convenient.

No. 10.

To Mr. Jennens.

Hearing you say that dear Mrs. *Jennens* wanted a Chain for her Watch, I beg she will accept of this from your most faithfull

Humble Servant,

S. MARLBOROUGH.

The Swiffalls lock to secure the Seals from being lost, and if she does not know how to open them, that Skill I can teach her.

No. 11.

To Mrs. *Jennens*.

Dear Mrs. *Jennens*, this is to desire that you will cutt me a Peice of Paper of the exact Bignesse of that half Hankerchare that you weare upon your Neck. I hope both you and Mr. *Jennens* are well. You will bee wellcome to dine here to-day if you happen to bee at Liberty.

Friday.

No. 12.

To Mrs. *Jennens*.

Mar. the 20th.

I give you many Thanks, dear Mrs. *Jenings*, for the Favour of your Letter, but I am in so great a Hurry, and have been ever since I had it, that I could not send to you, and now I am going out of Town. I wish, however, that you would just see how you like the Worke before you goe. I am sorry Mr. *Jenings* has been ill, for I wish both him and you all manner of Happynesse, and am your most faithful humble Servant,

S. MARLBOROUGH.

No. 13.

To Mrs. *Jennens*.

This is a Bitt of Cloath that came from *Hannover*, and did not cost above twenty Shillings a Skirt. I made *Dye* Frocks of some of it. I know 'tis not to bee had here, but I send it you that when you goe to *Chyn* you may bee so good as to see any Cloath that you like, Yard broad, and it need not bee finer than this. I shall want 22 Yards 3 Quarters, and half Quarter to finish this great Work of 14 Frocks. When you are out I wish you would fit me a Peice of the deep blew Thing that you thought would bee good enough to imbroader old Silver upon. I am ready to pay my Debts when you will ; let me know what they are. I wish you and Mr. *Jennens* liked to dine with us to-day at 3 o'Clock.

For Mrs. *Jennens*.

No. 14.

To Mrs. *Jennens*.

I was in great Pain for the Uneasynesse you suffered last Night, dear Mrs. *Jenyns*, from the Folly of my Servants, but I hope I shall hear by this Bearer that you got Home without any Accident, which is the chief Occasion of my Writing ; but now I have a Pen in my Hand I have a Mind to explain more fully what I ment about the Lace, which I should never have taken the Liberty to trouble you with, but that you were so good as to encourage me to doe it. I think it would look well to have the Lappits all Lace when the Hood behind is to be Muslin ; and therefore I desire you would bee pleas'd to order the Woman to make the Lace of the Breadth of the Lappits that you turned up to joyn at the Topp of the Hood before. That Breadth will be very hansome tell it comes to the Sid of the Hood. I mean that goes up from the Corner to the Croun, and then it will bee as well to have it narrower in any Way as the Lace falls conveniently. And you may order the Woman to take what Terms is necessary to doe it well, and bring it to me when it is don. I hope the fresh Air will establish Mr. *Jenyns's* Health, and that when you come to Town again I shall have the Satisfaction of seeing you, which is always a Pleasure to your most faithfull and most humble Servant,

S. MARLBOROUGH.

No. 15.

To Mrs. *Jennens*.

Thursday Night.

They tell me just now that there is a Doe come from *Woodstock*, which I desire you will send for to-morrow Morning. I dare not trust any Body to bring to you, for fear they should impose Fees for what came for my own Use. I hope you are well, dear Mrs. *Jennens*, and I wish Mr. *Jennens* were so to. I have been making formall Vissits all Day, and can hardly hold a Penn in my Hand, it has so tird me.

No. 16.

To Mrs. *Jennens*.

This narrow Fring is enough to put upon the Feet Base of the Bed, and if the broad can bee made to do the two side Bases, they are not seen at the same Time that the Feet is seen, and if it is a little narrower I think it no great Matter. I say that because I fancy they may make it up of near half the Breadth it is now. Six Feet is wanted for the Feet

Bases, and 14 Feet for the two side Bases, and as much more as it will take up in putting one. It is to lye upon the Damask which requires the less thicknesse. I shall want galloon of these two sorts to lace the Curtains, and to turn the Chairs and Window Curtains. May ask what they will do it for an once. You will observe the fine Colour of the Gold ; 'tis being the best duble guilt which makes it last so long, and look so well, for this has been made this eight Years at least. I hope you are better of your Cold, dear Mrs. *Jennens*, and that Mr. *Jennens's* Spirits are not so low as they were Yesterday. I am sure I wish you both all the Good in this World. I am in no Hast for anything but the Finery. This requires no Answer, but by Word of Mouth, to know how you doe.

No. 17.

To Mrs. Jennens.

This is the Collour of the Damask of which this Bed is made which I must match exactly, because it will be so fine a Fourniture. I shall want of it two Window Curtains, 12 Chairs, and four Curtains for the Bed ; but 'tis no Matter how long I waite for it.

No. 18.

To Mrs. Jennens.

I have tryd the Pattrons on the Bed, and find they will all three doe ; that you turned is the best and the prettyest, but any will serve very well. The little Bitt is broad enough, the longest Peice is the freshest Colours ; but of the two last Pattrons the Difference in the Price is only to be considered. If the Pattron you turned can bee had for a small Matter in Price more than either of the others that is best, but bespeak which you will, for any of them will be handsome, and what I call the best is full broad enough. If you and Mr. *Jennens* are not engaged to Day it will bee a Pleasure to me to have your Company at Dinner, but I love you too well to desire you should come unlesse you like it, dear Mrs. *Jennens*.

Wednesday Morning.

No. 19.

To Mrs. *Jennens*.

I give you the Trouble of this Letter, dear Mrs. *Jenyns*, to prevent any Mistake, and to let you know that I found a very great Change in poor Mr. *Guydott* for the worse Yesterday ; and I am sorry to hear this Morning by Mr. *Guydott* that he thinks him soe ill. I beg of you that hee may take Mr. *Walter Rawley's* Cordial at Night, and in the Morning, for it did certainly doe him a great deal of good once, and can doe him no Manner of Hurt ; 'tis what I have taken when I have had very little Complaint, and I am sure he wants Spirits extreamly ; and I still hope his Weaknesse may be recovered by that and Ass's Milk ; but since the Time they gave him over I never thought him soe ill as Yesterday. I hope your prity Son is well, which I desire to hear by Word of Mouth, and pray don't trouble yourself to write.

No. 20.

To Mrs. Jennens.

Wednesday.

I was in Hopes to have had a better Account of poor Mr. *Guydott* to day, but they told me hee was just as hee was. Tis very melancholly to indure soe much Pain, without knowing from what Cause, without which Nothing but an Accident can put an End to it; and certainly his Constitution (though a very good one) can't hold out much longer. Pray, dear Mrs. *Jenyns*, let me know what you think of him now. I don't remember that Mr. *Guydott* was ever ask'd if his Pain was just as beefore he was cutt, or if it is from the Wound. I am ever most faithfully yours,

S. MARLBOROUGH.

S:ʳ *Walter Rawley's* Cordial.

The usual Dose is a very large hazel Nutt, but in Mr. *Guydott's* Case he may take more, and three Times in twenty-four Hours.

No. 21.

To Mr. Jennens.

August the 22d, 1710.

I take the Liberty of sending you two printed Papers which seem to have a great deal of Strength in them, and confirm me very much in the Opinion I had before, that it is of the last Consequence to *England* to have a good Election for the next Parliament; and in that View I desire the Favour of your

Assistance in behalf of Sir *Philip Parker*, who is the Son of an old Friend of mine, and for whom both my Lord *Marlborough* and my Lord *Godolphin* would speak to you if they had an Opportunity. I am very sincerely, Sʳ, your

Most faithful Servant,

S. MARLBOROUGH.

My humble Services to Mrs. *Jennings*. I hope your pretty Son is well.

No. 22.

To Mr. Jennens.

Windsor Lodge, Dec. 4th, 1710.

Going out of Town sooner than I intended hindered me from desiring the Favour of seeing you and Mrs. *Jennens* at my Lodgings, which I hoped to have don; and not being certain when I shall have the Satisfaction, I take the Liberty to trouble you with the inclosed Papers, and at the same Time to tell you some little Part of my Story, tho it is a Subject that I have been very silent upon when under great Provocation; but I think it is more than human Nature can bear to see oneself cryd about the Country for a common Cheat and Pickpocket by a Man that is paid by the Ministry to do it when I have acted such a Part as I have don to her *Majesty*, and have so full a Justification as I have in all Perticulars in my own Power; and I would appeal to you or to any human Creature whether there ever was so scandalous a Reflection upon any Government as to have a Man encourag'd and paid for writting all manner of Lyes and malicious Insinuations of a Man that has done the *Queen* and the Nation such true Service, and when most People that I consult with seem to think his Services are as necessary yet as ever. And to make this Proceeding all of a Peice monstrous, I am credibly informed that tis Mr. *Pryor* that writes the *Examiner*, who has great Obligations to Ld. *Marl.*, and that Mr. *St. Johns* or Mr. *Harley* see it before tis printed. You will remark what the last says in his Letter to me of the Abhorance he has for publick and private Ingratitude exercised to my Family; but I think it was not then at such a Hight as now. What is write upon the saving such a Summ in the Robes seems so improbable that I never would have told it but that it may certainly bee proved; and as to those private Benefits I have had of the *Queen*, besides the great Summ the Lady's Woman has cheated in that Account of the Privey Purse, I can't resist telling you more upon this Occasion, which I hope you won't wonder at, that when the *Queen* came to the Crown, having playd with her forty Year agoe, and been her Servant six or seven and twenty, before which Time she did me the Honour to make a publick Profession of her Friendship to me, which I have never done the least Thing to forfeit. And upon these Considerations, when the late *King* dyed she told me she had Nothing in her Power to give like former Princess's, and therefore desird me to accept (in these very Words) of two thousand Pounds a Year out of the Privey Purse, which I might lay up, and supply in Time past what she wanted Power to doe. To this you may easyly imagin I replyd with all manner of Expressions of Thankfullnesse, but with all I said I had enough and my Sallarys were a great deal, and I would by no means take it. After that she was pleased to write to me to take it, and either own or conceal it as I liked best, for she did not care who knew what she gave to one that she could never reward enough ; but I still thought it too much, and I could never persuade myself to take it, which the Accounts will prove, as the *Queen's* Letter does the kind Intention ; and I doe solemnly protest that notwithstanding all the Envy of People upon that Account, neither publick or private, I never had the value of a Fan of her *Majesty* since she was a Queen more than my Places, which I came naturally and honestly into (and have endeavoured to serve her as well as any Mortal could doe), except, what Everybody knows, this Lodge, and the Ground to build a Hous upon in St. *James's Park.* And now I am upon this Subject I hope you will have so much Patience as to let me explain the Advantage of them, since the *Examiner* has magnified them so much ; and indeed I did once take them for great Favours ; but as to this Lodge, the whole Parke can witnesse that I don't make a Shilling of it, or take away the little Advantages from Keepers, most of which have many Children ; and what could be so wretched as to take what I don't want to make others be half-starved ? For the

Ground in St. *James's Parke*, a French Woman
had it for many Yeares in Quiet, and without Expense or any Merit that I know of; and I very well
remember that when my Grant was passd and the
Rent fixed to the Crown, Mr. *Woods* hee did not
think I had a good Bargain, being obliged to pay so
much Ground Rent and to lay out twelve thousand
Pounds upon a Lease that was to return again to
the Crown; and since the Lease was made I have
paid two and twenty thousand Pounds for that
Building, and before I can use it must pay ten more
at least, which I believe will answer any but the
present Ministry upon that Head. My Children
the *Queen* has been very kind to, but that I can
shew was of herself, and proceeded from old Promises; and being all marryd into great Familys, her
Majesty can't be injured by any Favours she has
don them; it has been no Wrong or any sort of
Injustice to any Body, and I hope their Husbands
are all as capable of serving her *Majesty* as any of
the Nobillity. For the building of *Woodstock*, without
doubt it has cost a great deal, but there was the
Authority of the Parliament for it, as there was for
Pension upon the Post Office; and upon that Account the *Queen* having the Concurrence of the
Parliament, I think it so far from being a Reproach
that it will bee a lasting Honour to my Lord *Marlborough* and to his Posterity; tho as the Building
will never be finished at *Blenheim* it can never bee
any Advantage or Pleasure to my Lord *Marlborough*
or his Family, but will remain now as a Moniment

of Ingratitude, instead of what was once intended; and for the Profits of the Parke, valued by the *Examiner* at forty thousand Pounds, I doe assure you the Balance of the last Account I saw for one Year was 47 Pounds; and tho five thousand a Year is certainly worth a hundred thousand Pounds in most Countrys, I believe no Body would give that Summ for any Pension that is subject to be paid, or not, as the Saucage Maker pleases. I hope you read the *Medley*, or you will think me madd for that Expression. I have now gone through as much of the *Examiner* as concerns myself, and it would take a Volum to contradict all the Lyes hee says of Lord *Marlborough*, which are known to bee so by so many People that I hope the Vindication is unnecessary. I can agree to Nothing but the Emperor's Favours, which were certainly very great, and the more to be valued because hee has had no ill Treatment from him, nor never was reproached with his Presents, but to shew English Gratitude, and I am sure I have Reason to be very thankfull for the Jewells, because I have no others to make myself fine if I would goe to the Assemblys; and after what I have said I would not have you or any Body think I am not very well satisfyd with my Fortune. You see I was that when I had not so much, since I refused the only Bounty that ever I was offerd; and my Fault not being Vanity (whatever else I may bee accused of), you may believe I am very easy with such Employments, so easy that I can part with them whenever it is proper, and that

I think is a good deal to say in an Age that Men born to great Estates will profess Friendship to People and murder them in the Dark, or any Way to get their Employments.   I believe such a Letter as this you never had, and the more Appologys I make the longer it will bee, therefore I will end when I have begd your Pardon for it, and assured you that I am very sincerely your most humble and most obedient Servant,

S. MARLBOROUGH.

I take the Liberty to send you a Doe, which I hope will prove good ; and if it does, I like them better than Bucks.   I desire you would not return these Papers, tho I think they would come safe by a Keeper ; but keep them for me till I come to Town, for the Letter from Mr. *Harley* I would always keep ; and if you know any Body that is worth convincing, who has a wrong Opinion of these Matters, you may shew them to any Body that you please.   I think no Body can blame me for it after such Usage.

[*From Mr. Harley to the Duchess of Marlborough.*

Thursday, Aug_t y^e 8, 1706.

Madam,—I miss'd the Opportunity of paying my Duty to your Grace last Time at *Winsor*, which occasions you the Trouble of this lre.   My Brother having made a State of yor Grace's acco^t, desird that I woud receive your Pleasure when you woud

permitt him to waite upon your Grace with it. I
perceive your Grace's Conduct will shine on all
Occassions, for my Brother tells me he has made a
Collection from all yr Accounts which have been
brought in for the Robes for 46 Yeares, since ye Yeare
1660, and by that it will appeare upon ye Comparison
how much better for a great Vallue yr Grace has
manadgd for the Crown. He will have the Honour
to present this to yr Grace whenever you please to
appoint a Time to receive it. I was just going to
send this Trouble when I was honourd with your
Grace's Command, which I shall apply myself to
obey with all imaginable Cheerfullness and Diligence.
I cannot think of a Servant and a Spy without the
utmost Abhorrence, pticularly when I find it levelled
at yor Grace's Ffamily, to whom we all owe so much.
I have been often provokd to see so much publick
and private Ingratitude exercisd towards ye Duke.
I shall not omitt any Thing which may tend towards
a Discovery of this Villany, and I will not put it into
any one's Hands, but manadge that myself. I beg
yor Grace will do me ye Honour to believe me to be
with ye utmost Duty,

Madam,
Yor Grace's most humble
And most obedient Servant,

Ro. Harley.]

SECTION SECOND.

HIS Second Series of Letters commences with the Duchess's arrival at Maestricht, a city of the Netherlands, whither the Duke had gone some time previously. The Duchess dwells with natural exultation and pride in some of her Letters, it will be seen, on the signal marks of distinction and honour bestowed upon the Duke in his progress through the Low Countries, and in some parts of Germany. These honours and regards must have been highly gratifying and consolatory to both their Graces, under the humiliating circumstances of their reluctant, if not their enforced exile.

No. 1.

To Mr. Jennens.

Maestricht, feb. the 12th, 1712.

I don't doubt but you heard that I got safe to *Ostend* in a few Hours after I left you, and my chief Reason of writing to you now is only to thank you for your good Nature in coming to *Dover* with me. All the Places one pass's thro in these Parts have an Air very different from *London*. The most considerable People I have seen have but just enough to live, and the ordinary People, I believe, are half starvd; but they are all so good and so civill that I could not help wishing (if it were possible to separate the honest from the guilty) that they had the Riches and the Libertys that our wise Cittyzens and Country-men have thrown away, or at best put in great Danger, and that they were punished as they deserve to bee by an Arbitrary Prince and Warr, as these poor People have been for fifty Yeares; and tho the Generality of them I have seen are Roman Catholicks, they fear the Power of *France* so much that they drink to the Protestant Succession, and the Honours they have don me in all Places upon the Duke of *Marlborough's* Account is not to bee imagined, which is not disagreeable now, because as it cannot proceed from Power, it shews that hee made a right Use of it when hee was General, and is a short Way of letting you see what People must think Abroad of this Ministry and Parliament. I write this by a sure Hand, and it being so uncertain whether Letters by the Post will come to your Hands, I shall not trouble you without I have some perticular Occasion of writing. I desire you to present my humble Service to Mrs. *Jennings* and Mr. and Mrs. *Guydott*, and to believe that wherever the Fate of *Marl.* and I am, you have two very faithfull Friends and humble Servants.

S. MARLBOROUGH.

No. 2.

To Mr. Jennens.

Aix, the last of *March*, O. S. (1712).

I hope you have received both my Answers to your Letters before now.   This is only to prepare you for the Trouble you will have from *Cox* whenever you have the Goodnesse to go to St. *Albans.* I find by a very foolish Leter that he has written to the Duke of *Marlborough,* that hee will tell you that hee can take his Oath hee has paid the four hundred Pounds he is charged with over and above what hee acknowledged to bee due, and hee adds that hee allways gave up his Accounts and Vouchers, and tis impossible for him to remember Things of that Time 12 Yeares.   I need not repeat to you what you will find in his Accounts, which you have or will examine, when you will see that all his Demands are allowd, tho ever so unreasonable, and some without Vouchers.   I hope you have a great deal of Patience, for I am sure the Businesse the Duke of *Marlborough* has given you requires it; but for my own Part I never am provoked so much at any Thing as at scummy and confident Nonsense, of which I never saw so much as in this Man, and I do hope you will not suffer him to impose upon you any new Cheates, for hee has bought a good deal of Land with what hee has allready got out of the Woods, and all Manner of Abuses in his Power, not being worth a Shilling when hee was made Bailiff. You will find him very desirous to defer this Matter

till the Duke of *Marl.* returns, but there is no Sense
in that, for hee has had the Interest of his Mony
many Yeares, and tis high Time to make an End of
it ; and since, as wicked as hee allways was, the
Duke of *Marlborough* did not let him manage his
Estate without some shew of an Account, Nobody
that hee can bring to speak for him will say that hee
can be allowd more than hee himself has thought
fitt to charge in Accounts that seem to bee raisd as
high as tis possible in all Perticulars. Since I have
Room I can't end without giving you some Account
how I pass my Time in this Place, which is in visit-
ing Nunnerys and Churches, where I have heard
of such Marvells and seen such ridiculous Things
as would appear to you incredible if I should set
about to describe them, tis so much beyond all that
I ever saw or heard of in England of that Religion
which I am apt to think has made those Atheists
that are in the World, for tis impossible to see
the Abuses of the Priests without raising strange
Thoughts in one's Mind, which one checks as soon
as one can, and I think tis unnaturall for any Body
to have so monstrous a Notion as that there is no
God, if the Priests (to get all the Power and
Mony themselves) did not act in the Manner that
they doe in these Parts, where they have three
Parts or four of all the Land in the Country, and
yet they are not contented, but squeeze the poor
deluded People to get more, who are really half-
starved by the vast number of Holydays in which
they can't work, and the Mony they must pay when

they have it for the Forgivenesse of their Sins. I
believe tis from the Charm of Power and Mony
that has made many of our Clergymen act as they
have don ; but my Comfort is, tho a very small one,
that if by their Assistance all are quit undon they
will not bee the better for it, there is such a vast
Number of Priests that must take Place of them,
for in one Church where I was lately there were 27
jolly-face Priests that had Nothing in the World to
doe but to say Mass for the living and to take the
dead Souls the sooner out of Purgatory by their
Prayers. My humble Service to all your Family
and to Mr. *Guydott's.*

No. 3.

To Mr. Jennens.

March the 20th, O. S., *Aix.*

I received the Favour of yours of the 10th upon
Thursday the 19th, and I am sorry you have an
Ague, which I fear will return, notwithstanding your
obliging Expressions, or my Wish's, which are, and
will allways bee, made for your happynesse of all
kinds. I had once that ugly Distemper ; and I took
a great deal of the Jesuits' Powder, which I hope
you will not bee averse to, for I am confident it
never did any body any Hurt, and the Physicians
have a better Opinion of it from their Experience
than they had formerly, and give it for many Things.
My Lord *Galloway* told me himself that he took it
all the Year round steept in Wine, and thought it
the best Bitter in the World for the Stomach. The

other part of your Leter the Duke of *Marlborough*
should answer ; but since you have address'd it to
me, I will take this Opertunity of commending myself (at the same Time that I return his humble
Services and Thanks) in saying that I am sure that
Nobody ever took so much Care of his Concerns as
you doe, except your humble Servant, and now I
will tell you what I know of these Matters.   There
is a very good new Hous upon the late Purchase
of *Parke Berry* : whether that is sufficient to serve
both Farmes, if a Tenant can bee had to take the
Whole, I can't judge, but I believe the old Hous
does not require so much to bee don to it as you
have been told.   For the Repairs that are wanting
at *Ustwick*, I never saw that Estate, and I am apt to
think, by what I did observe, that the Person that
sold it would lay out as little upon it as was possible.
For *Sandridge*, I doe know that the Duke of *Marlborough* did lay out near fifteen hundred Pounds
in repairing the Farmes upon that Estate, and you
may bee sure hee was told it was doing it once for
all, and that the Leases should oblige them to leave
them as they found them.   And you will observe in
the Accounts of *Coxe's* that there has been Bills
payd (which I put a stop to for the Future) without
any Body's Order, for Repairs ; and one Thing more
you will take for granted, that the Gardiner, *Middleton*, will always bee ready to lay out Mony upon
that Account, and much more Mr. *Carter*, tho I
think him a good honest Man, but tis impossible
for one that has nothing to live by but repairing of

Hous's to bee against the Duke of *Marlborough's* laying out Mony upon that Head, so that I am glad you begin to talk of going to *St. Alban's*, that you may see your self what is reasonable to bee don, and for your Reward I hope the Change of Air will doe you Good in your Health ; but when you conclude I hope you will make a Contract and tye them fast ; for whatever their Estimates are, they will exceed so very much, and that I know by woeful Experience. I have formerly given you the Character of *Coxe*, so I need not prepear you to take Care of him ; but this I will say, that hee will never come to any Conclusion that is honest or tolerably reasonable unlesse hee is frightned. I answerd yours concerning Mr. *Auberry's* affair as soon as I received it, which was very naturall when one is so sensible as I am of the Friendship you shew upon all Occasions to your most faithfull and most humble Servant,

S. MARLBOROUGH.

No. 4.

To Mr. Jennens.

frankford, the 14th of *May*, 1713, O. S.

I received the Favour of yours of the 10th of Aprill since I came to this Place. I did not make Hast to thank you for it because there required no perticular Directions in Affairs that you and Mr. *Guydott* understand so well, and are so good and kind as to take Care of ; but I want more than ever to hear from you, becaus you complaind so much of your being ill in your last Leter. I am come just now from a Window from which I saw a great many Troops pass that were under the Command of P. *Eugene.* They paid all the Respects as they went by to the D. of *Marl.* as if hee had been in his old Post. The Men lookd very well, and had buck^m and french Peices on, which they march with, I suppose, to use them so that it may be more easy in the Day of Battle. They had all green Bows in their Hatts, which is their Mark of Warr ; and the french they say have white Paper, on which they have write their own Conditions. Truly, after being beaten for ten Yeares, to see so many brave Men marching was a very fine Sight, but it gave me melancholly Reflections, and made me weep ; but at the same Time I was so much animated that I wishd I had been a Man that I might have ventured my Life a thousand Times in the glorious Cause of Liberty, the Loss of which will be seen and lamented too late for any Remedy ; and upon this Occasion I must borrow a Speech out of *Cato :—' May some chosen Curse, some hidden Thunder from the Shores of Heaven, red with uncommon Wrath, blast the Men that use their Gratitude to their Country's Ruin ;'* and to secure which bring in the Prince of *W.* and the Power of *France,* after turning out the Father, to preserve our Libertys and Religion.

When I had write so far I was calld to receive the Honour of a Visit from the Elector of Miance. I fancy hee came to this Place chiefly to see the D. of *Marl.* His shap is, like my own, a little of the fatest, but in my Life I never saw a Face that expressd so much Opennesse, Honesty, Sense, and good Nature. Hee made me a great many fine Speeches, which would not bee well in me to brag of; but I can't help repeating Part of his Compliment to the Duke of *Marl.,* that he wishd any Prince of the Empier might bee severely punishd if ever they forgot his Merit ; and the Civillitys are so great that are paid him by all sorts of People, that one can't but reflect how much a greater Claim he had to all manner of good Usage from his own ungrateful Country. It would fill a Book to give you an Account of all the Honours don him as we came to this Place by the Ellector of Sonnes, and in all the Towns, as if the D. of *Marl.* had been King of them, which in his Case is very valuable, because it shews tis from their Hearts ; and if hee had been their King hee might have been like others a Tyrant. The Ellector of Miance told us that all the Ellectors and the King of Prussia had taken their Resolutions to assist the Emperor as much as was in their Power in this just Warr ; and surely he must have been most barbarously used to goe on with it when *England* and those that they have forced have left his Alliance. There is an Account promis'd in French of his Reasons for going on with the Warr, and of all the Proceedings of our Ministers, which are very scandalous. The News Leters say here, that they have taken Care in *England* that they shall not bee made publick. Does not that smell rank ? The Facts are not to bee told. I write in a great Hurry, but I must say one Word respecting the Wood in *Sandridge*. I believe the Duke of *Marl.* will like whatever you and Mr. *Guy-dott* doe in that or Anything else, but I advise that great Care should be taken that non is cutt but what is orderd, which is the great Danger in those Matters. My Service to dear Mrs. *Jennens*. Pray write no more to me with Ceremony.

No. 5.

To Mr. *Jennens*.

May the 16th, N. S., *Wednesday*.

I write to you last Post, and since that I have the Favour of two Letters to thank you for, which I doe from my Heart, and will trouble you with no more Compliments; but one Thing I must say which perhaps you may think odd to come from me, that you are certainly the best Friend in the World except myself, for I am sure that I could go all over the World to serve one I professed a Friendship for, or that obliged me half so much as you have don, and I think you have don Meracles in my Affairs, for before I had your Account, when you said you had more than a thousand Pounds of mine, I thought you designd to present a poor Pilgirham. The best Friends that ever I had in my Life were poor Lord *Go.* and Mr. *Guy.*, both happy themselves to be out of this bad World, but for ever lost to me, which I can't pass without drooping some teares. The first of these Men managed the chief Part of my Mony; and I had great Trading in Stocks and Company, but I never sold Anything in my Life without

loosing by it till this Time that you have been so
kind to manage for me, and I have at present Tallys
for severall thousand Pounds that were once in
Lord *Godolphin's* Name, and now in his Son's, that
are upon Funds that are deficient, which is no great
Matter considering how near I think wee are to a
Spring. I believe you have heard that the Fortune
which that good Man had when hee dyed was about
fourteen thousand Pounds in Tallys, besides the
Godolphin old Estate under some Engagements, and
something more than seven thousand Pounds of
those Tallys were mine. The greatest Part of the
Rest belonged to other People, by which you will
see playnly what you believed before, how honest a
Man he was that had been so many Yeares, in three
Reigns, in the Treasury; and indeed he might truely
be compared to *Aristides* for his Honesty and Care
of the public Good ; and after giving his whole Time
to that Service you have seen how he was used, and
the Sorcerer who has ruin'd the Nation, and committed all manner of Cheates and Abuses, has been
extolled above all Men living, which has often made
me think that if it were not for the Satisfaction of
one's own Mind, as far as it concerns this World it is
much better to be wicked than good. You judge
very right in the Character you give of the Person
you were so kind as to invite to your Hous, for hee
is truely honest, and modest to that Degree that I
am ready to fall out with him for the same, for
'tis unnecessary to have any Ceremony with People
one lives so much with, and he is really what a Man

should bee as to Religion, perfectly good and just in all Things, without imposing Superstition and Nonsense, which can bee of use only to Hypocrits or Fools ; but I feare there will allways bee a vast Majority of such as long as the World endures. I am not uneasy as you think upon Account of the Time that is so heavy as you imagine me, which you may the easyer believe because I us'd to run from the Court and shut myself up six Weeks in one of my country Hous's quit alone, which makes me now remember Mr. *Cowley*, who says 'tis very fantastical and contradictory in human Nature that People are generally thought to love themselves better than all the Rest of the World, and yet never can indure to bee with themselves ; and hee adds that it allways shocked him to hear one say that they did not know how to spend their Time, which would have been very unlucky and ill spoken by *Methusalim* ; but tho' I have quoted what suited my part very well in that Author, and that I love Solitude more than ever, I would not have you think that I don't wish earnestly to see my Friends, and to be in a clean sweet Hous and Garden, tho' ever so small, for here there is Nothing of that kind, and in the Gardens, tho' the Heges are green and pretty, the Sand that goes over one's Shoes is so disagreeable that I love to walk in the Road and Fields better, where the D. of *Marl.* and I go constantly every Day in the Afternoon, and stop the Coach and go out wherever wee see a Place that looks hard and clean. 'Tother Day we were walking

upon the Road, and a Gentleman and his Lady went
by us in their Chariot who wee had never seen before, and after passing us with the usual Civilitys,
in half a quarter of an Hour or less they bethought
themselves and turnd back, came out of their Coach
to us, and desired that wee would go into their
Garden, which was very near that Place, and which
they think, I believe, a fine Thing, desiring us to
accept of a Key. This is only a little Tast of the
Civillity of People abroad, and I could not help thinking that wee might have walk'd in *England* as far as
our Feet would have carryd us before Anybody that
we had never seen before would have light out of
their Coach to have entertaind us. I have had an
Account of Lord *Nottingham's* Speech in the *Hous
of Lords*, with the Story of the Treasurer to *Harry*
the 6th. The Aplication of it was delightfull, and
I am confydent I should have been the greatest
Hero that ever was known in the *Parliament Hous*
if I had been so happy as to have been a Man; but
as to the Feild, I can't brag much of that sort of
Courage, but I am sure no Mony, Tittles, nor
Ribons should have prevaild with me to have betrayd my Country or to have flatterd the Villians that
hav don it. I am charmd with my Lord *Nottingham*;
I believe there lives not a more worthy Man, and I
hate myself when I reflect how much I was once im-
posd upon in thinking otherwise of him, which was
certainly without any reason ; and I am so much convincd of that Error that, as I said before, if I were that
happy Creature Man, I would never differ from him

in one Vote as long as I lived. This long Letter
upon Nothing will make you think that tis no Wonder
my Time does not lye upon my Hands, since I can
employ it so idly, but that is no Argument for my
troubling you so much, for which I ask your Pardon.

No. 6.

To Mr. Jennens.

March 12th, O. S., *Aix-la-Chapelle.*

I did not receive the favour of yours of the 20th
Feb. till Tuesday, and I was told it had been sent
first to *Frankford*, by what Mistake I don't know.
I have so many obligations to you upon the Duke
of *Marlborough's* Account, as well as upon my own,
that it would be an endless Thing to enter upon that
Subject, and my Letter is likely to be so long upon
an other Account that I shall only beg of you to
imagin all that a gratefull Person is capable of in
wishing to return so much Goodnesse, and believe
that is in my Heart, tho I can't expresse as I would.
As to Mr. *Aubery's* Affair I desire you would bee
pleased to make an End of it in whatever Manner
you think fit, but to take the Trouble of reading
what follows, which is to vindicate myself as much
as for your Information, and particularly in what
relates to the Date of the Bill, which is of so long
standing that it certainly intittles him with justice to
have raised his Prices if it had been my Fault:
therefore I desire you will send to Mr. *Hodges* and
ask him before Mr. *Aubery's* Face if I had not sent
him severall Times to the late Mr. *Aubery* as well as

to his Son for my Bill, which I never could obtain
till after my last Charriote was made, which was
some Time after I was in *Marlborough Hous*, and it
being very extravagant in all Respects, and different
from his own Estimates, and some Things charged
which I thought I had paid, the Proofs of which I
could not presently find, I only ordered him Two
Hundred Pounds upon Account till I could look for
all the Papers that were necessary to shew him in
order to the Abatement of his Bill, which, tho the
Date is old, if you observe there is Nothing of any
great Value when the Deduction is made of what
hee either charged twice, or should not have put
to my Account.   The first Thing being a little
ordinary Chaise with one Horse, I finding all the
Inside and Frames, and yet hee had no more
Conscience than to charge it at 30 Pounds.   The
next Article worth mentioning was a very plain
travelling Coach that was to bee of the same
Dimentions of One his Father had made for Fifty
Pounds, and for which I have his Father's Acquittance, and according to what other People pays I
had no great Bargain, since the Painting inside and
Glasses must make that come up to more than four
score Pounds, and Mr. *Boscawen* said his Coach that
we used to *Dover* was but Sixty the whole Charge
of it : this is enough to know how ill he would use
me ; but he can urge Nothing against his own
Estimate and his Fathers Acquitances, which I
thought he had seen, because I remember very
well that hee sent me his Reasons in Writing how

he came to make that Mistake in a double Charge
that hee found his Father's Accounts in great Dis-
order. This Paper I have under his own Hand, I
suppose, that is, it came from him; but he seems he
has found a way to make it all appear right in his
Books now. I can't be positive how long 'tis since
the Panniling of my Coach was made, lined with
Green, which is the first Article of his Bill of any
great Consequence, and that Coach being now in Use,
I am pretty sure it can't be more than Four or Five
Yeares old at most, so that what were before in that
very old Date is for Repairs, as hee calls them, of one
poor Coach that his Father made new, and that was
very seldome used for some Yeares, for Part of the
Time when the Duke of *Marlborough* was Abroad
I had no Horses, using a Chair in Town, and the
Queen's Coaches upon most Journeys; and when I
was a Summer or two in *Oxfordshire* hee knows I
had only a Dutch Berlin that was quite new, and
that hee never saw till lately that I sent in to have
another sort of a Carriage with high Wheels.

No. 7.

To Mr. *Jennens*.

frankford, the 17th of *June*, O. S.

I have receivd the Favour of yours of the 12th
of *May* upon the first of this Month, and I hope you
have recoverd all your Illnesse, tho you mention
nothing of it, and I wishd to have read in the first
line that you were very well. I did acknowledge
that from *St. Alban's*, which I don't doubt but you

have received before now, and the Duke of *Marl.* had one from Mr. *Guydott* as hee was going to *Mendleham*, dated the 11th of *May.* I desire that you will let Mr. *La Guerre* have what Mony you think he deserves ; but I doubt hee has painted very little, since hee left it Five Weekes. I am very desirous of having it finishd, tho the giving all the Trade and Power to *France* does not look as though I should ever enjoy it. However, I have this Satisfaction wherever I am, that tho a Woman I did all I could to prevent the Mischiefs that are coming upon my Country, and having nothing to reproach myself with, nor nothing in my Power that can doe any good, I am as quiet and contented as any Phylosopher ever was, but, at the same time, if I were a Man I should struggle to the last Moment in the glorious Cause of Liberty ; for if one succeeds tis a great deal of Pleasure, and if one fails, tho one looses one's Life, in that Case one is a Gainer, and when one considers seriously tis no matter how or when one dyes, provided one lives as one ought to doe. I am contented to hear of my *St. Alban's* Affairs, because it gives me the satisfaction of your Leters ; but otherwise you might spare that Trouble to yourself, and say only you had orderd what was right ; for the Lady that you waited upon for the Mony I would not be uneasy to her, and if you desire her only to take her own Time in sending to you, I believe it will be enough. I hear, tho I am at this Distance, that a thousand Lyes are set about of me, but it gives me no manner of

Disturbance. Nay, the *Examiner*, when I happen to see it, does not in the least afflict me, for I fancy whoever can take such Papers would write them if they could, and therefore he does not add to one's Enemys, and I was really pleasd to see such a Man who write the 'Tale of a Tub' made a Dean just after the pious Recommendation.

No. 8.

To Mr. Jennens.

Oct. the 27th, O. S., *Antwerp.*

I received Yesterday the Favour of yours of the 13th of this Month, which was fuller of the Spleen than ever I am, tho I am uncertain whether I shall ever see my own Country again ; and Nothing can bee imagind more disagreeable than for one to live abroad that speaks nothing but *English*. But you know at Pickitt you have wone a Gaim when those you playd with were 47 to non, and I think Nobody that can do any Good should dispair so much as to throw it up before it is quit lost, since Nothing can bee worse than that. At the same Time it must bee allowd that wee are in a very sad Con-dition, considering the Power that is given to the King of *France*, the Ignorance and the Corruption that is now in *England* ; and yet sometimes I can't help having some small Hope that Men with solid Fortunes will not submit tamely to bee given up to *France* ; and if that should happen, surely there is yet Strength enough in *England* to save the intire Ruin of it, tho Ages can't recover the Mischeifs that

our present Government have don. You seem to
desire my poor Opinion not only in my own smal
Affairs, but in yours as to the disposing of Mony,
which makes me ready to laugh; but if you would
really have me speake, I can't think that you are
more obnoxious then any other Person in the Kingdom. I wish all were in the same Condition, for
tis not necessary for you or I to make use of all wee
have, and for my own Part I should be very well
contented to live out my short Span of Life in any
of my country Hous's. This is a World that is subject to frequent Revolutions, and tho one wish's to
leave one's Posterity secure, there is so few that
makes a suitable Return that even upon that Account,
which is the greatest Concern, one need not bee unhappy for Anything that is not in one's Power to
help. I am of your Opinion as to Bank Bills and
all publick Funds, though at this Time I hear they
don't fall; but they will sink all at once, I suppose,
when there will bee no Buyers. However, I know
Nothing that is better, for I have seen Nothing
abroad that does not look so poor, that I can't fancy
Securitys here, where one knows, nor understands,
Nobody; and if *England* won't open their Eyes and
struggle before 'tis too late, the King of *France* will
bee in Time Master of the World. But perhaps I
may dye before all the Misery comes that 'tis so
reasonable to apprehend, which will put an End to
all my Concern. I would fain have had the Duke
of *Marlborough's* Directions in answering that Part
of your Letter that relates to him; but all that I

can get him to say is, that he leaves all to you ; that
hee thinks Nobody can desire to sell an Estate but
according to the Rent it will make yearly, and that
the Way you took concerning Mr. *Trocher* was right.
That 23 Yeares' Purchase was high, but that must
bee according to the Markett Price. Mr. *Reeves* is a
Man of so ill a Reputation that I can't think his
Interest was Anything in *Woodstock* till hee made
himself usefull to some by the Service hee was in ;
and before another Ellection can come there 'tis
probable that the Duke of *Marlborough* will have
no Strugle in it, or that hee will give all Things of
that Nature over. But since Mr. *Reeves* has been
sufferd to cheat so long, it will bee noe great Addition to his Abuses if you let him alone till you see
the Effect of the Petition against Mr. *Cadogan*. I
suppose one of the first Things that will bee endeavoured will bee to turn out all the Members that
will not blindly vote whatever they are orderd
against the Interest of their Country ; and if *Torys*
that have Estates and are not for the P. of *W.* will
not lay aside Party so far as to assist those that
would help them in saving the Nation and all that
is now left valuable in the Country, it is Time
indeed to despond and throw up the Cards, which I
was so much against at the Beginning of this Leter ;
and I hope the Case is not so desperat as to bee
past Recovery, if People that have Sense, and
Fortunes, would but consider what is truely their
own Interest. I will write to *Hodges* to goe to Mr.
Elliott, for I think hee is honest, and above getting

such a Summ as is demanded from his Nephew ; and hee having given me the Acquitance in full, and assuring me that I owd Nothing at that Shop, I think 'tis his Businesse to sett that Matter right. I don't know what to say to the Debt at *Woodstock* but that I never knew that I had any, it being my Manner allways to pay *Hodges* whatever he layd out. I have Bills for every Journey that ever the Duke of *Marl.* or I made to that place from *Hodges*, and for all those Sort of Things one can have from a Grocer's Shop. I am sorry you complain of Want of Health, which I fear *London* will not mend ; but when I read further, where you desire me not to think of putting more of my Concerns into your Hands, I could not bee sure that you were not quite weary of them, tho' there is a great many very kind Expressions mixd in your Leter. All I can say to that is that I am sure I had much rather suffer as wee have don in our Fortunes for Want of a right Management than give you an unreasonable Trouble of any Kind ; much less would I prejudice your Health ; but for putting Anything I don't use into any other Hands, I must beg your Pardon, for if you won't take Care of it for me it shall ly dead in Mr. *Edwards's* Hands, who never did Anything for me like improving, but receivd my Mony and keept it till I drew Bills upon him ; and I have lately sent for near four hundred Pounds, part of which was to get a Jewell I had lost, and to recompense an inno- cent Servant that had been put into Prison about it, and that was so inocent that it gave me a great deal of Trouble when I saw hee had been wronged. The Description of *Newmarkett* is as melancholly as those I give of my Travells, when such a Man as you mention is the chief Support of that Place, who was a Begar many Yeares agoe. I think it ridiculous to write News to you, and yet I believe you can't know anything concerning *Dunkirk* so true as I do, having lately seen a very honest and sensible Man that was there. Hee says that there is some Show of demolishing it, and the Men have worked three Weeks, but now fall sick, and it does not advance much; and 'tis a good While since Orders came from the *King* to fit out his Ships to Sea and evacuate; but the 31 *October*, New Style, there were no Kind of Preparations for it, and really I think it were doing the Ministers great Wrong to believe they design to destroy that Place effectually, after so many Tricks as they had to avoid it, which if it is ever don must proceed from Necessity, and the King of *France* fearing to loose some of his Friends in *England* before he has compassed all he desires. Tho', let it happen as it will, I believe Nobody will say that his *Majesty* has not had a very good Bargain, since 'tis certain that our Treaty with *Spain* is not yet signed, which I have allways heard was the chief Cause of the War. You make Excuses for a long Leter, but what should I say for all this Wisdome who know so very little and can doe less? Pray give my most sincere Service to your Wife.

No. 9.

To Mr. Jennens.

July the 20th, N. S., *Antwerp.*

Between Businesse and taking leave of the
People of this Country I have but just Time to
thank you for the Favour of your last, I don't know
of what Date, and am so hurryd I can't look ; but
you said you were allready weary of the Penn, but
so kind as to think of writing me, which is a Trouble
I would prevent this terryble hott Weather; and I
hope you will rather keep yourself quiet in good
Air, that you may have Health to come to me at
St. *Alban's*, where wee intend to go in a very few
Days after wee come to *London.* *Friday* next wee
sett out from this Place, which will bee the 16th
English Style ; and we design to be at *Ostend* in two
Days, and to embarke for *Dover* the first fair Wind.
I am faithfully just as I ought to bee, and a sincere
Friend to dear Mrs. *Jennings.*

No. 10.

Memorandum.

Whereas I have desird and directed *Rachel* Lady
Russell to pay the Interest of ten thousand Pounds to
Robert Jennons, Esq., and also the Tenants of a lease-
hold Estate at *Aguy*, in the County of *Kent*, to pay
him their Rents as they become due : I hereby direct
that the said *Robert Jennons* shall and do dispose
thereof as the sam shall be paid to him, or as

Opportunity shall offer, for my Cost in purchasing
Bank Stock or any other Stock or Government Securi-
ties or otherwise, and in such Manner as he shall think
fit; and do agree that if any Loss or Damage shall
happen in the Disposition thereof, that the same
shall not be born by him, the said *Robert Jennons*,
but by me, my Executors, Administrators, or Assigns,
and that the said *Robert Jennons* shall be indemnifyd
for whatsoever he shall do of or in Relation to the
Premisses. Witness my Hand this twenty-sixth
Day of *January*, one thousand seven hundred and
twelve.

S. MARLBOROUGH.

No. 11.

To Mr. Jennens.

Pray doe me the Favour to send to M. *la Guerre*,
a *Frenchman* who is now painting the Hall at *Marl-
borough Hous*, and let him give Mr. *Guydott* an
Acquittance for fifty Pounds upon Account of the
Work, which hee will be pleased to charge to the
Duke of *Marlborough*.

I have not observed that any of my Leters have
been opend. However, I think tis better when they
take that Fancy that they should be put to the
Trouble of guessing from whom it comes than to
put your Name.

No. 12.

To Mr. Jennens.

feb. the 21st, O. S.

Tho I have non of your Letters to answer, nor nothing of any Consequence to say, I hope you wont think me troublesome that I put you in mind of me, having so good an Opertunity of writing to you. We have had no News since the 9th of this Month from *England*, and I am very impatient to hear how *Her Majesty* boar the Journey to *London*, for upon that I think all our Happynesse depends. Those small Hopes I had of your Knight are now vanishd, since I hear hee says the Ministers dont design the P. of *W.*, and that there is no manner of Danger of him. My Lord *Straford* speakes the same Language at the *Hague*, and swears to it upon his Honour, which hee often did to make People easy in this most advantageous Peace, and the great Care the Q^n would take of all her Allies. Mr. *Bromley* to I hear has sent his Son to the Ellector of *Hanover*, and Cousin though he bee no doubt carrys all the Assurances imaginable from Sr *Roger*, who is so honest a Man that it must have some Effect upon the El., who never read the History of *Monk*, and really I think it is not easy to believe there is such a Man in the World as Sr *Roger* till one has paid for it by one's dear bought Experience. All these Reflections put me into a deepe Melancholly, for I am thoroughly convinced that if Sr *Roger* can by his Witchcraft and the Majick of his Wand deceive and quiet these honest Torrys that would

E

not ruin their Country, they will never have another Opertunity of saving it after this Session of Parliament; but you say it will be Happynesse when wee are out of the worst Condition in the World, which you think is Uncertainty. *Drayden* I know is of that Mind, and says tis better once to dye than allways fear. But that is against Mr. *Cowley*, who says,—

> Hope, of all ills that men endure,
> The only cheap and universal cure.

And I own I begin now to bee in great Apprehension of Misfortunes that can't end but with my Life. I am sorry to hear the Soldiers are sent for from *Ghent*, because I am confydent it is only to disperse them if they can't break em, that they may bee said to bee out of the Way of doing any Good in Case of an Accident. Prince *Eu.* is returning to *Rastad*, which I conclude will end in a Peace and give the King of *France* more Liberty to serve the P. of *W.*; tho in one Part it will expose our Ministers Conditions which they made for the *Emperor* the $Q^{n's.}$ dear Allie, when she had all the Power in her own Hands, for there is no doubt but the King of *France* submits to grant your Conditions to the *Emperor*, or *P. E.* would not goe back.

I take this safe Opertunity to desire that you will tell Mr. *Guydott*, with my humble Service, that hee should pay the Five Hundred Pounds a Year to you that is in his Name, which hitherto he has let Mr. *Edwards* receive, and with the Rest of my Mony you will bee so good as take Care of it. When

you write by the Post I think it would not be
amisse if you made use of this Cypher only to avoid
Names. For my own Part I dont care what the
Ministers know of me, since they cant hang me
while I am on this side the Watter, and I seldom
direct a Leter by the Post that has anything in it,
so that if they open them they cant be sure who
they are to; but tis not impossible but they may
know your Hand, and sometimes I think you are a
little too free with them. You see by this how
much easyer it is to give Advice than to take it,
and I suppose will laugh at my Wisdome. My
most humble Service to your dear Wife, and pray
let me know if there is any thing in these Countrys
that I can serve her in; Netnet and Lace and Table
Linnen, and Holland, I believe, is much cheaper
here than in *England,* and if she will employ mee,
pray asure her that I will take as much Care to
serve her well as I did the *Queen,* who I had the
Honour to save a Hundred Thousand Pound in
nine Year, which I can prove to any Body. I am
told that there is about Fifteen Mile from this Place
Guilt Leather that is very good, and not above
Half a Crown the dutch ell square. I have not yet
seen it; but if either Mrs. *Jennings* or you like any
thing in this Part of the World, no body on Earth, I
am sure, has a better Heart to serve you, and if you
could think it a trouble pray remember that you
have paid me before hand for more Service than I
fear I shall ever have it in my power to doe you so
long as I live, notwithstanding all my good will. I

generally write a Leter to you after I have taken leave, and yet I have allways more to say.

CYPHER.

queen	.	.	.	I	Elector of H. . . 14	
lord treas.	.	.	2	Mr. Jennings . . 15	
Ministry .	.	.	3	Du. of Marl. . . 16	
hous. of Lords	.	4	Sa. Marl. . . 17	
hous. of Com^ns.	.	5	L^d. Sunder. . . 18	
Citty of London	.	6	L^d. Anglesey . . 19	
S^r. Tho. Han. .	.	7	Torrys . . . 20	
Mr. Bromly	.	.	8	Whiggs . . . 21	
mony	.	.	.	9	Mr. Cadogan . . 22	
sickness .	.	.	10	Craggs the father . 23	
death	.	.	.	11	L^d. Nottingham . 24	
King of france	.	12	Scotch lords . . 25	
P. of W. .	.	.	13		

No. 13.

To Mr. Jennens.

Feb. the 14th, O. S.

I give you many Thanks for your very chearfull Leter of the 12th of this Month, tho I must own I cant see much Reason for it. The best Thing I have heard is that those Men who have been so bold in betraying this Country have been much frightnd of late, but I have heard that some of them were never counted very valiant, and tis the Nature of Cowards, I believe, never to think they have Security enough when the least Danger appeares; but if Men of Fortunes in the Citty, and Parl., and Country would all arise to save their common Libertys, I do believe it might yet be don, tho by all the Missagess to *France* and the Accounts one has from thence, it will not bee long in their Power. But I am intirely of your Mind that wee shall soon bee out of the Pain of Uncertainty. I wish I could as easyly believe that I shall bee contented when I have lost all, and am forced to live the rest of my Life in these durty Countrys. I am now in some Doubt whether my Phylosophy will goe so far as that, tho it has been sufficient to support me against all that the worst of Men or Wemen have don, and tho I know one shall bear whatever one can't help, I pray most heartily that I may not be tryd any further, for tis quite another Thing to hear that one is never to see *England* nor one's Children again, at which Time they will not bee in a very good Condition, then it is to leave a disagreeable *Court* when one knows one has not deserved ill Treatment, and only to make a Sort of a Pilgrimage for a little while, hoping to see Justice don upon some of one's Enemys. I am told Sir *S. H.* will bee the Speaker, and I hope it is not impossible that hee may do well, if he can think it for his Interest to bee for the Protestant Succession rather than for the P. of *W.*, for he has never yet acted upon any good Principle I am sure ; but whoever will help to save us from *France* I will forgive their other Faults. I was this day put at Ease for poor Lord *R.*, and I wish with all my Soul that your Son may quite escape that terrible Desease, or that it may pass as well over. I will answer the Businesse of your Leter by the Post, being in a mighty Hurry now; but I had a great Mind to tell you by this safe Hand that I am ever most faithfully yours, and the dear Lady's that has promisd me one of her Cotages.

No. 14.

To Mr. *Jennens.*

Jan. 25th, O. S.

I have write to you so often and so much since
I had any of yours, that I should have Nothing to
say but Repetition of Thanks for all your Goodnesse
to me. But Lord *G.* having proposed to the D. of
M. the lending a great Summ to the D. of *B.*, which
I believe had been don if it had not been for the
difficulty that Mr. *J.* made in lending under six per
Cent., I can't resist writing my Thoughts upon this
Matter, and giving you my Reasons why I would
not have to do with those two Dukes in Mony
Matters; and you will be pleased to acquaint Mr.
Jen. with what you think proper out of this Leter;
and I will begin it with telling you that I know a certain Person who at the Revolution clear'd a Mortgage upon his Estate to a Man that had lent it in
King *James's* Time, and was forfeited in King *William's*. It was a Man of near as great Quality as
his Grace of *B.*, and before that Action had a much
better Character; and I can't help thinking that if
another Revolution happens, of which wee are in
such manifest Danger, that the D. of *B.*, who will
have some Pretensions of Merit, is as likely to make
himself easy in his Debt to the D. of *Marl.* as
most Men that I know. I have stated what I
think is likely to happen if the P. of *W.* is put upon
the Throne, and if hee is not I can't see that such a
Man as the D. of *B.* is likely to be more easy in his

Fortune, which will make it so troublesome to get
the Interest; and you know some People don't care
to have to do with Peers, who have great Privileges
to defend themselves against the Law, which they
seldom fail of making use of, when they have no
Honour, or when they are so simple as not to know
what a Principle is; and as for his Grace of *G.*, who
is to be concerned for a small Part of the Interest,
I beg leave to tell you upon this Occasion what I
know of him, by which you may judg whether it bee
reasonable to go out of the common Way to oblige
him.   When this present *Queen* came first to the
Crown the late Lord *Sunderland*, who had don her
many Services in a very hansome Manner in King
William's Time, came to mee and desird that I
would ask her when *Q*. *Dowager* dyd to give him
two Lives in a Forrest in *Northamptonshire* which
was very convenient to his Family, because it gave
him Oppertunitys of obliging his Neighbours there.
Her most gracious *Majesty*, with all the Pleasure in
the World, granted this Request, and acknowledged
very readly that hee had deservd a great deal
more from her.   My Lord *Sun.* dyed before the
Queen Dowager, but when that happend I carryd
the Paper to the *Q*. of what she had promisd him,
upon which she said it should bee made good to this
Lord *Sunderland* and to his Son; but before the
Patent was passed my Lord *Featherston* and the
present Duke of *Grafton* both pretended to have a
Right to the same Thing, one from his dead Mistresse, the other from King *Charles*, upon which her

good *Majesty* orderd that their Cases should be given to the *Attorney-Generall*, who was then S.ʳ *C. Northey*, and that hee should give his Opinion whether either of these Lords had any Right to the Forrest. S.ʳ *C. Northey* (who has shewn himself no Friend to that Ministry or to my Family) said that they had neither of them the least Pretention; that the Q.ⁿ had full Right to give it to whom she pleased; that their Pretentions were rediculous; and the D. of *G.* in one Part absurd, for hee had Something in that Country from the *Crown*, which made him more improper to have the Forrest than any other Man, because in having that hee would bee a Check upon himself. I believe by this Time you are satisfyd that the Q.ⁿ had a Right to dispose of this Thing, and if she could give it to any Body, she might justly perform her Promise to my Lord *Sun.* I was then her great Favourite, and did the Drudgary of the Place. The Duke of *G.* nor his Family deserved no more then any other of the Nobillity from the Q.ⁿ; and for myself I never had the least Obligation to him or to any of his Relations. However, I consented to deferr the Passing of this Grant, so very convenient to my Family, till Something happend that might be rather more pleasing to the Duke of *Grafton*, and when I had obtaind that from his Grace the Forrest was to bee given to Lord *Sun.*, and my Grandson after him; but before this was compassed the Sorcerer got Possession of the *Crown*, and the D. of *Graf.* had so little Regard to Honour or to what I had don (who could have securd this

Thing to my Family for so many Yeares together without the least Reproach), that hee made use of the Sorcerer to get this Forrest without any more Ceremony, and diverted himself, as I was told, how much he had disappointed me and my Grandchildren. This is all Matter of Fact, and the material Part of it any Body may know the Truth of from Sir *C. Northey*. I would not have you think from this Account that I am angry with the D. of *G.*, for I have met with so much ill-Usage, and have seen so much of the Worthlessnesse of the Generality of the World, that I have very little Resentment against any Body ; but I must confess I am not yet so good a Christian as to love my Enemys, or to desire to serve such Sort of People at my Lord *Marlborough's* or my own Expense. And if you please you may read this Leter to any of the Trustees. Two of them I have told my poor Opinion of this Matter to allready. The last Post brought us the News of Sir *George Byng's* being put out, which can bee for no Reason but that hee prevented the P. of *W*. landing in *Scotland*, and Sr *Wishart's* Squadron being augmented (who is a professed *Jacobite*) shows that the Ministers will not be frighted again as they were lately in case wee should bee so unfortunate as to loose so good and wise a Woman as the *Q*ᵗ, whose Answer to the *Irish Hous of Commons* I conclude is not so much for the Sake of the *Chancellor* there as to warn the *English Parliament* that they must not presume to find Fault with any of the Proceedings of the

Ministers in *England*. But how miserable must
that Nation bee that S.ʳ *J. Hanmere* is the Hope of,
which I hear hee is stiled, and that hee said himself
that he deserved from his Country, when all that
I can remember of his Merit is that hee has sup-
ported the Sorcerer to break the best Alliances that
ever were made, and had the most glorious End,
and his last great Action was in making a fine
Speech in favour of the Trade, and the next Day
managd an Address to the *Q.ⁿ* quite contrary to what
he had proposed!

No. 15.

To Mr. *Jennens*.

Jan. the 22d.

I have thankd you for the Favour of yours of
the 31st *De.* some Time since, which was the last I
received from you; and since that I find by my
Accounts sent from *England* that I have about four
hundred Pounds to dispose of, which I have a Mind
to keep a little While, to see if it will not bee of use
to me hear, for I really think our Prospect is very
deplorable; for let the Sorcerers give out what they
will of Mrs. *Morley's* good Health, it is next to impossible that one with such a Complication of Dis-
eases can continue long; and by the Accounts I
have from *England* they are putting the Fleet and
all the Power into the *French* Hands. At the same
Time I am now satisfyd that the Sorcerer has made
Propositions to the Q. of *H.*; but that is only a
Copy after *Monk*, whose Character is a very ill one
if rightly represented in a little Book I have lately

read ; but perhaps the Author, to make the Comparison the greater between him and S.ʳ *Roger*, may have been too hard upon *Monk*, but I am sure no Pen can express the Villany that the later is capable of, who is all Things to all Men, still with a Design to ruin them ; who has broke the best Allyances that ever were made, and for so glorious an End, and is now endeavouring to ruin the Laws, Liberty, and Religion of his native Country, after which I think hee may pretend to bee sole Minister of State to the *Devil*.

I am ever most faithfully yours and your dear Wive's. This Leter comes by a save Hand inclosd to my Hous Keeper.

No. 16.

To Mr. Jennens.

Jan. the 14th, O. S.

I have received the Favour of yours of the 31st of *De.*, in which you acknowledge one from me of the 5th of the same Month. I think I write one since, but I write so much that I really can't remember my own Dates, but I allways acknowledge yours and then burn your Letters. I believe the Way I have sent my Letters to you has come safe ; but I will keep this a Day or two by me to send by a Gentleman that is going to *England*, since I have Nothing to write that requires Hast. As long as Mr. *C.'s* Cause depends on the P., 'tis not good to disoblige Mr. *R.*, or anybody in those Parts ; but when that is over any way, I believe there wants some good Method to be taken in that small Affair, and I am sure nobody living will do it better than yourself, nor with more Kind-nesse to the D. of *M.* I think in my last Letter I said that Mr. *Cadogan* would never make use of the Lodg in *Woodstock Park*, and that the D. of *Marl.* did not intend to keep any thing up there for the use of any Gentleman. The Keepers, to bee sure, are in a strang way, but I fear Mr. *Rivers* being put over them will bee only making him a sort of a Tyrant, and they will all agree in helping one another to cheat. I have heard quit contrary (and from a very good Hand) from what you hint concerning a young Gentleman's being a Protestant ; but 'tis certain that my Lord *Myddleton* has left him, and is gon to the.Q^n, his Mother; and a strang Creature that is called a Protestant, Mr. *Higgons*, whos Sister you have seen in *England*, is made Secretary to the P. of *W.*, which, to bee sure, is some good Advice from *England* to shew what a Love he has to Protestants, tho he would loose three Crowns rather than be One himself; but this is so very simple that I can't think hee can doe much Hurt. I wish we had not other Things to fear, and that which I dread most of all is the Power of *France*, which by our villanous Ministry is sett up so high, and the Treaty is not yet signd with either the *English* or *Dutch* between them and *Spain*, but in such a Manner as signifys Nothing, which I suppose is the Reason that one heares no Mention of it from *England*. The two *Dutch* Ambassadors came to see the Duke of *Marl.* in their way to Paris, and my

Lord *Essex* being a Boy and very well acquainted
with one of them, Monsr. *Buys*, made all the Company laugh very much by asking him first if their
Treaty was signed with *Spain*; to which hee
answered (out of conscience), 'No!' 'Then,'
replyd Lord *E.*, 'you have given *France* all, and
you still depend upon them. I wish to God your
Son and I had made this Peace, which I am sure
wee should have managd better;' and severall
Things passd that made every Body merry, tho I
think tis no laughing Matter.

If I guesse right you mean in having more
Games in View than one. I must take leave to
differ with you, for I am sure there is Nothing
intended by any in the Ministry but bringing in the
P. of *W.* at any rate; and tho Sir *Roger* has
deceivd many as to that Design, it has been plain
to me for many Yeares: first of all, when the *Q.*
was Princesse I heard a Man that was a great
Friend to Sr *Roger* say by Chance without the least
Design that hee valud Himself upon his Father's
having had a great Hand in the bringing in of
King *Charles.* Then I observd when hee was
very much relyd upon by poor Lord *Godolphin* hee
perpetually prevaild with him to put Men into
Employments, and do Kindnesses for Men that
were known Friends to the Interest of King *James*,
for which L^d *Go.* had many Enemys. The other,
like *Monk*, all the while professing to bee of another
Principle, and to my certain Knowledge, as soon as
hee had Opertunitys of speaking to the *Q.*, hee did

all the ill Offices imaginable to the Hous of *Han-nover*. All these are very ill Symptoms in one that was to fix the Revolution Settlement, and I know a hundred Remarks that I made and put together which made it plain to me when nobody else would believe any perticular Design of Sr *Roger's* but that hee was undoubtedly a tricking Knave. I entertaind myself Yesterday with a little Book called the *Art of Restoring*, which I conclude you have seen, where an Account of *Monk's* Proceedings is well exposd, and which I never saw before. But I think my Lord *Treasurer*, who is there, Sr *Roger* has copyd after him in most Things ; and I am confydent hee has no other Game in View then to follow his Example, and that may either increase or at least secure his Fortune. In reading this Account I found one Line of a Leter of Generall *Monk's* that Sr *Roger* had exactly copyd in one to L^d *Go.* ; which Leter hee gave me to carry to the D. of *Marl.* when I went to the Sea Side to meet him, and I have it still. This I mention only to shew you that Sr *Roger* was taken with *Monk's* Expressions, and, like poet *Boys*, made them his own. But in one Thing he has been honester then Genl *Monk* was to the Parliament, who took so many solemn and false Oaths ; for I could never find that hee has made any Professions to the Ellector of *Han.*, and this must proceed from his thinking the other Game sure, since hee has never scrupled doing an ill Thing, nor stock at any Lye upon any other Occasion. But what hee has don concerning the Succession in the Hous of *Hannover* has been only to deceive the Publick, and at the same Time hee had not thought it necessary to treat that Family with common Decency.

My best Wishes attend dear Mrs. *Jen.* I don't name her when I write by the Post, because it may give a Light to shew who my Leters are to if they are opend at any Time. I think you are not so cearful as you might bee in such Matters, for in your last, perticularly by the Post, you spoke of your Cousen *G.*, which shews as plain who the Leter is write by as if your Name was at it. The Reason that my Leter that you mention was so long before it came to you, I believe, was because it was One that I sent to my Hous Keeper to carry as directed by Mr. *Harney*, who was long upon the Way. But I have write by the Post since, which I hope you received; and I will never send you any Leter but that way, or, as this comes, by a very safe Hand. You seem still to desire my Notion as to puting out Mony, but you must needs bee a better Judg that are upon the Place; and all I can say is that the *French* are so strong, and all in Power are such worthless Wretches, that if I knew where I could put my Mony safe abroad I would draw every Shilling out of *England*; but Mony in *Holland* is not above three per Cent., and that Country can't subsist long after the villanous Ministry have given *England* up to *France*, which one Way or other will soon happen, I believe; but since I don't know how to secure any Thing, when all is lost I hope some

of my Friends will keep me. I shall want but very
little, and I hope I shall not trouble any Body long,
since I think 'tis much better to bee dead than to
live out of *England*. I write to Mr. *E.* two months
agoe that I might know what Mony he had of mine,
and never had any Answer; and last Post I write
to him again ; when I have his Answer I shall know
whether the Summ is worth troubling you with.

No. 17.

To Mr. Jennens.

De. the 5th, O. S.

Soon after I had written to you I received the
Favour of yours of the 16th *Nov.*, which shewd me
that I was in the right in thinking I had write at
least one Leter that was not acknowledgd by this
Time. I imagin you are in Town, and I hope in
good Humour, tho as to the Publick I can see no
Reason for it. I saw a Leter to day that gave an
Account from *Frankford*, and from a good Hand,
that the first Demand of the French *King's* Generall
upon Prince *Eugene* was to have Satisfaction for fifty
Millions in their Mony, which I think they say is five
in ours, for the *King* his Master's Expence in this
last Campaigne ; and as soon as the poor *Emperor*,
like the rest of our Allies, is forcd into a Peace, tis
easy to see that the French *King* may do whatever
he will with *England* ; and really considering that
Spain is now given away by our Ministers, and not
to bee recovered by the *Emperor*, if he could get any
tolerable Conditions for himself, I think it is not

very naturall for him that is a mighty zealous Catholick to strugle, if it were in his power, to prevent our having a Popish King upon the Throne, tho hee might bee useful to us on that Poynt while it was his own Interest as well as ours.   I believe I gave you some Account in my last of *Dunkirk*, which is just as it was to all Intents and Purposes as for any Advantage to *England*; and I was told yesterday by a very honest Man that the Risband is three quarters of a Mile from the Harbour, which is demolishing it only according to Seur Juggles Desire ; but I believe this is a Repetition, and all I can say upon that Subject will bee so, and therefore I will go to an other, upon which perhaps the Truth may not yet have been told you, that tho the Treaty was signed with *Spain* on *Saturday* last for the Commerce, it was with such Restrictions and Circumstances that makes it the same as if it was not, for four principle Articles are left to bee settled by Commissioners, and the Spanish Ministers have signed with a Protestation that with regard to all the other Articles their signing shall not bind them unless approved on by the Court at *Madrid*, by which you will see that tho the World is given to the King of *France*, *England* has nothing till Commissioners have settled it, which is to bee first reported by an ignorant Commissioner of Trade, and then approved of by the *P.*, both influenced by the worst Men that were ever before Governors of any Country.   Pray forgive me for writing so much upon Polliticks, which is the last Subject I should chuse if my very

Being did not depend upon a right Resolution taken
in this *Hous of P.*, not with one that it will bee in
vain to think of having in *England*. And tho one
submits to many Things with some sort of Patience
that can't bee prevented, I can't help saying that
living Abroad makes one very indifferent whether
one's Life be long or short. I was sorry to find by
some of the foreign Prints that they talk of marrying
the P. of *W.*, because while he was single the Accident of his Death would have made all quiet ; and
in that Case, if the hatefull Names of Whig and
Torry must be kept up, they could do no mischief
but vex one another. I have had an Account lately
severall Ways that my Lord *Peterborough*, having
taken the Name of *Smith*, passd in Disguise at *Basle*,
and had a long Conference with the P. of *W.* and
my Lord *Middelton*, and tis confirmed with so many
Perticulars and Certaintys that Nobody can doubt
it : and before the Thing come out I must add one,
that I know a Person that gave an Account when
he was at *Callice* that he sent the greatest Part of
his Servants another Way than that hee took himself, and hee went by no other Name but that of
Smith, even when he was at *Callice*. I don't suppose
that our Ministers have any Need of sending him to
the P. of *W.*, but his Lordship sees that tis a proper
Visit ; and as much as my Lord Treasr. seems to
despise Mony that is given so freely, I don't think
that my Lord *P.* would have had so much of it if
hee were not thought of some good Use, or one that
hee feares to disoblige. I am of your Mind that

there will never bee any Advantage made of the
Parke at *Woodstock*, and I hope Lord *Go.* will make
no Difficulty in using it in Anything that is a Pleasure to him ; but I am sure it must bee from your
Goodnesse that it must bee put in order. Mr. *Cadogan* is not here, but I will answer that Part of
your Leter concerning his Lady in my next. Mr.
Reeves will never pay without Law, to bee sure, but
I fancy hee has cheated enough to be in a Condition to doe it; for, as I have said before, hee has
made some Advantage by Cattle in so large a Place ;
but there are other Things that don't belong to that,
which is certain Rents. I believe soon after *Christ-
mas* I shall know what little Mony I have to dispose
of, and I am glad you have been so good as to allow
me to trouble you with it. All the best Wishes of
my Heart bee with you and dear Mrs. ——.

The Leter I have mentiond in this I believe
may not come first to your hands.

No. 18.

To Mr. Jennens.

July the 9th, O. S. (1713).

I have received the Favour of yours of the 29th
of *May*, and that of the 24th of *June* last Night.
In the first you desire to be restraind if my Inclinations are not the same of yours for venturing Mony
rather than locking up, in which I agree intirely ;
and I desire you once more to consult Nobody but
yourself in any Thing that concerns me, for I am
intirely satisfyd that you will judge well ; and when

I have don what is most reasonable, I am allways
content in Matters of much greater Consequence
than any Thing that you will have to manage for
me, which till *Michaelmas* it seems will be Nothing,
but about that Time I believe I shall add something
to it, having no Opertunity of spending any Thing
in this Place upon myself, I came so well provided
with all Things, and I can't reasonably dispose of
a Shilling upon my own Account. But when one
meets with People that are miserable, which I really
think in all Countrys is the best way of employing
what one can spair, allways taking Care not to depend upon any Body one's self. I reckon soon after
you will receive this Leter you will be taking your
Prograse, as you so kindly intended, for which I
hope you will bee rewarded with a good Health. I
hear the *Emperor* is very resolute in his Design of
carrying on the War, and I am told hee has a Scheem
for such an Number of Men as will be more uneasy
to *France* than is believd. But to be sure Nothing
can stand before the King of *France* long if *England* continues to assist him; and as long as this
Ministry continues I think there is noe doubt that
England will act what is most for the Advantage of the *French* in all Things, which must certainly a little sooner or later bring in the P. of *W*.
There is a general Muster made upon that Account,
for a Roman Catholick, who is very honest in his
way, was here lately, and told me hee had quited a
very good Provision for his Wife and Children hee
had under the *Emperor*, which the D. of *Marl.* in

compassion got him, his Estate having been sold in
Ireland by the Prots. ; and he can't have any In-
heritance in *England* or *Ireland* without another
Revolution.   I askd if hee was uneasy with any
Body in the *Emperor's* Service that hee left it, to
which hee very frankly replyd No ; hee was a Man
of great Vertue himself, look'd after his own Businesse, and would not suffer Injustice to be done by
any Minister to the meanest of his Subjects (and the
same Character I have had of him from severall),
but hee said he look'd upon the Restoration of King
James to bee so well laid that it could not fail, and
persuaded me as a Friend to try to bring the Duke of
M. early into it : to which I answerd, that having
don so much for the Cause of Liberty and for the
Good of *England*, I had much rather have him
suffer upon that Account than change Sides, for that
would look as if what hee did in the Revolution was
not for Justice, as it really was, but for to comply
with the Times.   This Sort of Conversation did not
please my new Acquaintance at all, but wee parted
good Friends, for tis naturall for a Roman Catholick
to act for one hee thinks his lawfull *King*, and very
tempting when hee hopes by it to recover a good
Estate ; but hee own'd to me that hee had been so
ill-usd in *France* after the Death of King *James*,
that if he were to begin his Life againe he would
keepe quiet at Home, and venture for Nobody, and
in this I agreed intirely with him.   But I still per-
sisted that if one must hazard, it should bee in the
Cause of Liberty, for if one was ruind for that, one

had the Satisfaction of having performed a right Part; and I was born with a great avertion to Fools and Tyrants, and I believe who ever is the first is in great Danger of being the last, which is not strang, for certainly those that have most Understanding will have most good Quallitys, and Fools are most capable of Flattery and of all Manner of Injustice; and they are generally very ill natured, for Want of Sense hinders them from being touched with the Sufferings of any Body, and having no Judgment to guide them, they follow their Inclinations, let them bee ever so wicked or foolish. You see what it is to incourage me to write, for I have taken a second Sheet of Paper, and when I come to the end of it I dàr say I shall still have a Mind to write on, though I can tell you Nothing from this Place that is worth writing. But tis enough to make me vain to find I was not so surprisd or mistaken as you were with the News of throwing out the Bill of Commerce; for tho I could not help taking some Pleasure that there was Quarrils and Variance among such Men, I thought it was plain by the Conclusion of a certain Knight's Speech that he did not divide from his Friends, that hee designd to espous the true Interests of *England*, but to get some Reputation in the Country, and to raise his Price higher by distressing the Ministers; and at the Time that my Friends were so delighted in *England* that they wrote me Word they hoped to see me very soon, I never doubted that all the Devices and Wheadles imaginable would be contrived to allure and sweeten the People, and amuse them, by taking care of their Trade, and all that they could think of to colour and conceal their knavish Purposes till tis too late for any Body to help by smugling. But I will own that even this Sett of Men, that have so near compassed the Ruin of *England*, have surprisd me in condemning the Bill of Commerce, and thanking for the great Care that had been taken of the Trade and Honour of *England*, all in five or six Days, it is needless to say that all these Mischiefs are brought about by Mony, and the People that were allways in the Service of the P. of *W.*; and I can't see what can hinder us from having just such another *Parl.*, with the methods that are sure to be taken. I never remember what I write two Days, but by your Leter it appears to me that it was something which makes you think me much better than I am upon the Account of my Country, and I am really so good as that I would not deceive any Body; and therefore I desire to explain myself, tho I shall not get so much by it as Sir *S. Har.* is likely to doe, whos Price now they say is *Secretary of State*; but I believe his great Passion is Mony, of which he has certainly had a great Deal. Now I will confess to you, tho nothing upon Earth could move me to doe what I thought an ill Thing, I believe my Vertue is not like Cato's, for my Concern is not for *England*, but for my Children and a few Friends and good People that are there. I fear there is not many, and if I would not bee in the Place of the most powerful of these

Wretches, 'tis for my own Sake purely, because my Notion is that they are of all Creatures the most detestable. I know one must dye some Time or other, and I really think the Matter is not very great where it happens, or when; but if I could have my wish it should bee in *England*, in a clean Hous, where I might converse with my Children and Friends while I am in the World; but if that must not bee I submitt, and I will own to you that I am not so much to be pittyd as some People, having never seen any Condition yet that was near so happy as 'twas thought. When I was a great Favourite, I was raild at and flatterd from Morning to Night, neither of which was agreeable to me; and when there were but few Women that would not have poysond me for the Happynesse they thought I enjoyd, I kept the worst Company of any Body upon Earth, and had Reason to be much more weary then of any that can happen. Still wee are like a Sort of banishd People in a strang Country, and I could say Something to every Part of my Life that would convince you that 'tis only a new Sceen of Trouble which few are free from in this World, and I thank *God* I can bear any Thing with some sort of Patience as long as I have the Satisfaction to know that I have not been the Occation of what is calld so great a Misfortune myself; and why should not I bear with any Misfortunes that happen to the whole Country as well as to me? But the Thought of this indeed is what touches me most, because that is for ever Destruction to me and all that I wish

well to ; but for anything else it is not worth an
Hour's Pains ; and I can eat

(Unfinished.)

No. 19.

To Mr. Jennens.

frankford, August the 30th, O. S. (1713).

I received the Favour of your Leter of the 7th
of this Month Yesterday, and I have a great Mind
to thank you for it, tho I am in some Hurry, being
to leave this Place to day and go to *Antwerp*, and
like sick People I am glad of any Change, though
this Place was better than *Air-la-Chapelle*. Many
of the Accounts that comes from *England* looks like
a Comedy, but I fear it must end soon in the Ruin
of all that is valuable, for by the Addresses of last
Post the People seem to be just as madd as at the
Beginning of this Ministry, by which I conclude that
wee are doom'd to bee as miserable in *England* as
they are in any of the arbitrary Countrys that I have
seen ; and it is brought about the same Way as
Denmark was ruin'd ; for a Lady Yesterday that
came to take her leave of me, who is a Subject of
that *King*, told me that they had once as good Laws
in *Denmark* as wee had in *England*, but that they
had a *Parliament* that made their *King* absolute ;
and then she made a very good Description of their
present *King*, who is very weak and wicked. You
are very good to take so much Care of the Painting
of my Hall, and I can never thank you enough for
that and a thousand other Things since I had the

Happynesse to know you; but I can't think I shall
ever live in it, and indeed I should be very well
contented with the worst of my country Hous's.
These are melancholly Thoughts, but when I consider how much of my Life is passed, and how little
there is in this World that is any reall Satisfaction,
I can bear with any Thing of this kind with more
Patience than you will easyly believe. When you
are so good as to write to me, your Leter will find
me at *Antwerp.* My Services to your dear Wife;
the Duke of *Marl.* presents his humble Services to
you. I wish he would write himself sometimes
because his Hand would not trouble you so much
to read; but hee is intolerable lazy, and has not
write once to any of his Daughters since hee left
England. Pray present my Services to your Friend
that you were to meet, and to take so much Trouble
with about the D. of *M.'s* Concerns. I received
the Favour of his Leter dated the 8th of *July.* I
am in such Haste I don't know what I write, and
can't read it over.

No. 20.

To Mr. Jennens.

Antwerp, Sept. the 26th, O. S. (1713).

Just before I left *frankford* I received the
Favour of yours of the 7th *Aug.* I thank'd you for
it; and since I came to this Place I have had that
of the 30th of the same Month, by which I am sensible that the Duke of *Marl.* and I have as kind
and good a Friend in you as I could desire, and I

hope you believe how great a Pleasure it would be
to me if I were capable of returning it, but that being
unlikely ever to bee in my Power, you will accept of
my empty Thanks, and believe them very sincere,
notwithstanding that Words are easy Things, and
that you have met no doubt with false Friends as
well as your humble Servant. But I must bee a
strang Creature if I were not for ever obliged for
the Pains you have taken in a Time when Friends
are very rare, that is in *England*; but Abroad,
wherever the Duke of *Marl.* goes all the People
continue their usual Marks of Respect and Affection
to him, which I conclude does not only proceed from
the Service he did to the common Cause, and the
good Usage of People that were in his Power, but
from the Knowledge that these Countrys have of
the Tyranny of *France*; and when *England* feels
the same, and from that repents of their ungrateful
Treatment of the Duke of *Marl.*, it will bee of little
Use either to him or to themselves, and I give
every Thing for lost since I have had an Account
that wee have, if it bee possible, a worse Sett of
Men for three Year in the new *Parliament* than
there was in the last; and they were chose in such
a Manner as shews there is no Law, Sense, or
Honesty left in that unhappy Country, which was
once so flourishing; and I expect to have this *Parliament* lay a Foundation of making *England* as
miserable as the rest of the World. As to what
you say of laying out the 600 Pound, I can only
repeat that I am sure that whatever the Event

should prove, I shall allways be satisfyd with what you judg best; and as dismall a Condition as *England* is in, I know of no other Country where one can place Mony that one can bee sure of having in again, no more than I know of any Person to trust that is like yourself. Therefore, pray doe allways what you like best with mine, and only tell me of it when you are at Leisure. I don't know yet what I have more to give into your Hands, not having had Time to inquire into those Matters, and I have been obligd to give and lend Mony to some that wanted since I left *England* ; and 'tis not to bee imagind how many miserable People by some Accident or other one meets with Abroad. It was once my own Inclination to venture a little in hopes of a great Return, but when I consider what the Ministers have don for the Interest of the P. of *W.*, and the Strength they have given the King of *France*, whatever Avertion the Generality of the Nation have to trust a Popish *King* brought in by *France*, I think many remote Things have a sad Prospect as to putting out Mony, for 'tis past a Doubt what is intended, and the Question is only whether this *Parliament* will bring him in, or, if they wont, whether the King of *France*, with the P. of *W.'s* Party, are not able to doe it by Force. In either Case it will end much alike ; but to be sure public Hands that are out of use to the carrying on of the Government will fail the first

(Unfinished.)

No. 21.

To Mr. *Jennens.*

Antwerp, Oct. the 8th, O. S. (1713).

I write to you since I came to this Place. I have
not much to add after I have thankd you for the
Favour of yours of the 22ᵈ of *Sep.*, by which I find
you have don all the Good you could think of in our
Affairs. I am glad you are so well pleasd with
Holdenby, because that was my Purchase for the
Duke of *Marl.* when he was Abroad, and now I
have promisd to buy it of him for myself, believing
that Land will bee the thing that wee shall enjoy
longest in *England,* for I believe our Government,
by the Advertisement in the *Examiner* concerning
the new Project for ceasing all Taxes in Time, is
some Design upon the publick Funds, which, without
any violent Injustice, must sink as soon as People
are convincd of the Design to bring in the P. of *W.,*
let it bee in whatever Manner they can propose. I
agree very readyly with you that *England* is one
of the best Places to retire in, and I have often
lamented that the Duke of *Marlborough* was not of
my Humour, and then hee would have stayd in it as
long as he could ; and as for my own Part I never
was and never can be concernd for any Thing that
ill People either say or act against me, and if I could
bee now in a Court as pleasing as the present is
disagreeable, I would never quit my dear Hous as
I have don, but I should bee glad to enjoy any of
my Hous's with my Children and a few Friends.

That was allways the Life that would have been my own Choice, and is now the Height of my Ambition ; but I have learnt to bee contented with any Condition that I can't reasonably endeavour to change. The inclosd Paper I made one here put into English out of a French Thing that had Nothing else worth taking Notice of, tho I am sorry to say this Part of it is true, that is, the *Queen's* Ministers had orderd it so that she really had the Appearance of the just Character that is given her in past Times. I am glad you enjoy so good a Health, which I wish you the Continuance of very heartily, and all Manner of Happyness to your Family, and to those for whom you are most concernd. The Duke of *Marlborough* presents his humble Service to you, and thanks for indulging him in Laisynesse in not writing. Pray make my condoling Compliments to the Lady that has lost her Father, when you have an Opertunity.

No. 22.

To Mr. *Jennens.*

October the 29th, O. S. (1713.)

I write to you so very lately, and I should not trouble you now but that Sr *Godfrey Kneller* has write to me to desire you will give Mr. *la Guerre* one hundred Pounds more, which hee says will make two hundred and fifty, upon his finishing the Hall, and hee said it would be don in a Week. Hee adds that the great Stair Case is about half don, and he commends his Performance so much that I have got the Duke of *Marlborough's* Leave to write to you

that you would please to order him a hundred
Pounds.   I have been much entertaind to day in
reading several of Mr. *Steel's* Papers, and Nothing
has pleasd me better a great while than S.ʳ *Walter
Raleigh's* Letter to Prince *Henry.*   You may remember what a Meracle I did with his Cordial upon
poor Mr. *G.*   I wish the Nation could tast his
charming Notions upon Government before 'tis too
late, tho I am confydent One might rase One from
the Dead sooner than One could make Mrs. *Morley*
sensible of Sir *W. R.'s* good Advice.

No. 23.

To Mr. Jennens.

No. the 29th, O. S. (1713).

I take the Opertunity of a save Hand to thank you
for the Favour of yours of the 7th of this Month,
which I received but last Post.   In that you acknowledge mine of the first of *Oct.*, but I fancy I have
write one since that ; perhaps I am mistaken, and if
I am 'tis no great Matter more then to let you know
that I had non of yours to thank you for when I
received this of the 7th : so much I am sure of.   I am
very glad you give so good an account of your own
Health, which I wish may continue where ever you
are.   I thank God the D. of *M.* is very well, and
I am so so.   I imagin you now in Town, and most
of the country Gentlemen in a great deal of joy at
the News that the Risband is blown up, and *Dunkirk* effectually demolished.   But as ignorant as you
may reasonably believe me in these matters, I can

asure you that there is nothing don in the Demoli-
tion of *Dunkirk* but according to the scheem of
Sieur Juggles, which no doubt was agreed upon by
our Ministers to see how the Nation would relish it,
and that has made them so outragious against M.^r
Steel. I have lately seen the plan of *Dunkirk*, which
was thorougly explaind to me, and you may depend
upon it that the Harbour is just as it was in the
time of the Warr to all intents and purposes, and
there is a Demonstration that they design to doe no
more to that, because at this very time the King of
France is making a Causway from *Lille* to *Dunkirk*,
which would be of no Use but to ship off their Goods
which used to goe to *Dunkirk* by *Ipres*, but that
Town is now in the Hands of the *Dutch*, to whom
they pay Custome, and to save that Mony they are
making this Causway, which so plainly exposes the
English Minister that I wonder hee had not a little
more Patience and Regard for the Men who have
given him the World when he was in Despaire. I
have lately seen a Gentleman that was in *France*
when a Knight was there who, I think, you had
once a good Opinion of. I wish he may deserve it
when the *P.* gets in, helping to save our sinking
Country; but this Man asures me that hee observed
that hee did not care to pass his Time with any but
the People of St. German's, tho the French made
great Court to him. I have been reading in the
Book that was so much talk'd of concerning the
hereditary Right of the Crown of *England*, and I am
come to that part where they show how a Prince

that has not that Right, yet may enjoy the Crown lawfully if the *Prince* who has the Right gives Leave. 'Tis not difficult to ghesse what that means, and I conclude that the whole turn of the Book is to shew that Somebody may have an Act to dispose of the Crown by Will, for you know one good Turn deserves another ; but I am at a Loss to reconcile the disposing of a Crown by Will to the Torry Principle, who have run madd upon hereditary Rights, and say the *Queen* is hereditary, because she is the first Protestant. Now if, after all this, *Parliament* may dispose of the Crown by Vote, what becomes of hereditary Right ? But after all there is Something so extremely rediculous in this Design that I cant believe it can pass. I wish it were as improbable that the P. of *W.* may have it some other way before she makes her Will. Pray present my humble Services and Thanks to dear Mrs. —— for her kind Remembrance of your humble Servant. What you mention of the Estate that was sold I wonder at, but I think it no great Matter. One does not know what is best to place one's Mony in with such a dismall Prospect.

No. 24.

To Mr. Jennens.

De. the 28th, O. S. (1713).

I have just now received your Favour of the 18th of this Month from *London*, in which you say you have received no Answer to yours of the 16 *No.*, which I wonder extremely at, because I

remember I sent one Leter by a safe Hand, and
having answerd all the Perticulars in every Leter
that ever I had from you, except what concernd
Mr. *Cadogan's* Lodge, I will not endeavour to repeat
what I have said till I am certain that they are lost,
for Fear of troubling you with Repetitions. But in
that case, if there is anything material to answer,
I must beg you to write again, for my manner is to
burn my Letters as soon as I have answerd them,
unless in former Times, when they came from such
as I feared would doe me some Mischief. As to
the Lodge, called Mr. *Cadogan's*, which to be sure
hee will never make use of, I believe it is the Duke
of *Marlborough's* intention that non but Keepers
should bee in that Parke, therefor 'tis no matter how
little is don to it, or whether Anything at all. I have
not time to speak to the Duke of *Marl.* before this
Leter goes, but I am sure he would have no Account
of Anything sent to him here, and that hee is intirely satisfyd with all that is don for him. Your
serious account of my great Estate made me laugh,
a Thing that does not happen often. But I hope I
shall have a little more to improve in a short time.
I believe it will be more necessary now to hinder
Mr. *La Guerre* from painting than to press him to
it, for I am told that in dark, dusky weather it is
not good to work, and that the Painting in damp
weather will not hold nor is ever good. I suppose
for that reason he will have leisure, but 'tis so much
for his own Creditt to have such a Work well finishd
that I hope hee will be carefull of it without much

looking after. The Conclusion of your Leter is very kind and very sanguine, and I am glad for your ease that you are out of the Spleen; but I confess I don't see what reason you have to think of our coming to *England.* All the Roman Catholicks say here, that the reason the King of *France* presses so much to make a Peace with the *Emperor* is because he would fain bee soon at Liberty to put King *James* upon the Throne; and I think the Intelligence which I have had of that kind must be good, since 'tis that *King's* Conscience, Glory, and Interest to have him there; and if that were not the Design, he would never give the *Emperor* so good termes, now hee is Master, as hee has allready offered, for he has receeded from several Things that our honest Ministers agreed to, particularly the great Advantages for the Elector of *Bavaria,* which is a new Infamy upon the *English* Government, but I fear as monstrous as all their Proceedings have been. Powerful Guineas when the *Parliament* metes will bring them off with flying Colours; and I suppose 'tis to make the Bargains that they are put off in so unreasonable a Manner. I am told that the People in *Holland* are very much allarmd, and that severall who were impos'd upon see their Errors, and are sorry for it. But I fear 'tis too late, and yet I doe believe fermly that if Men that have Fortunes of both Partys would aweak and bee active, that they might yet doe Something that would save us from some of the Mischiefs that the Sorcerer and his Allies are bringing upon us. I was told by a very honest

Gentleman that has been lately in *Holland*, that the Bishop of *London* told the Minister of the Duke of *Lorrain* that all the *Queen* expected as to the removing of the P. of *W.* was to have such an Answer as was fit to be rec^d, which this Minister told again to a hundred People ; for that Court have been so ill usd by the King of *France* that they hate him of all Things, and would not keep the P. of *W.* there if they could help it. Wee observe in some Accounts that the Duke of *Berwick* makes frequent Visits to the P. of *W.*, which 'tis likely is to satisfy him that whatever the King of *France* does with the *Emperor* it will prove to his Advantage, and when that *King* has joynd the Power of *England* and *Spain* to *France*, I think hee may bee contented to let the *Emperor* bee easy in these countrys that he now possesses ; and when hee is so, I can't see why a zealous Popish *Prince* should concern himself for base Hereticks when hee can't get by them ; and I suppose all Roman Catholick Princes will be threatend with Purgatory and Hell for ever should they offer to oppose so holly a Design, by which they may give the finishing stroke to Heresy. When I write this Leter I did not intend to send it by the Post, which has made mee blott out many things; being disappoynted of the Opertunity I thought I should have had, and I hope you will forgive me for not writing it over again ; 'tis the greatest Fault that I shall ever commit to you, but it had been greater if I had sent it as it was.

No. 25.

To Mr. *Jennens*.

Jan. the 28th, O. S. (1713-14).

I think my last Leter to you was upon the 25th
of this Month, and since that I have received the
Favour of yours of the 14th of *Jan.*, which has been
longer than ordinary upon the Way. What *Cox* says
of paying the Duke of *Marlborough* any Mony
after hee was put out of his Service is utterly false.
The D. of *Marl.* says that hee orderd him to be
pressed to pay in the Ballance of his Accounts often,
and hee still desird a further Time for it, and promisd as often that it should bee paid at this Time
and that Time, very faithfully to the Goldsmith,
and both *Hodges* and *Charles Middleton* can witnesse that hee made the same Promises to them
when I sent to him, which hee could not have don
if hee had paid that Ballance to the D. of *Marlborough* ; and just before I came away, I think hee
was in Town and had not then this new Invention,
which is the most impudent Thing that ever I heard
of, for I remember *Hodges* and I passed severall
hours in looking over his Accounts the last time the
D. of *Marlborough* was at St. *Alban's*, which was
after the Death of poor L$^{d.}$ *Godolphin*, and it had
been a very naturall thing for him then to have said
hee had paid the Duke of *Marlborough* so considerable a thing as that Ballance when hee was in
the Hous, and I am confydent pressd him for the
Mony himself, which hee then gave Assurances that

hee would pay in a short time ; and is it likely, besides all I have said, that hee would pay so great
a Summ without an Acquitance, when hee was
turnd out of the service, or that the D. of *Marl.*
would take it in that manner, who had so much
reason to bee disatisfyd with him ?   He asures me
that hee allways gave him Acquitance for any Mony
hee received.   I never had anything to do with him
but what *Hodges* and *Charles Middleton* knew of.
I suppose you have not forgot that I brought all his
Accounts to Town, finding that there were so many
Abuses in them, and I orderd M^r· *Wilson* to make
the whole Charge of all that *Cox* had received, or
ought to have received, since the time that the D. of
Marl. had signd the Book, which I think was in
1700 or there abouts ; and tho I did not much doubt
that there were severall Cheates in the former Accounts, I did not examine what was discharg'd, and
I thought it very moderate to *Cox* to allow severall
things that I believd Abuses in the time following,
and desired nothing but what appeard plain by what
he had receivd, and not so much as pretended to
have paid by his own Accounts either with or without Acquitances ; and in that manner the Account was
stated by M^r· *Wilson* at my leaving *England*, and I
am much surprisd that hee should make such a
mistake in it as 1,200 Pounds, to my Disadvantage,
upon this occasion.   I must tell you one Perticular
of *Cox*—(tho tis not very necessary to look for more
Proofs of his being a very great Rogue), which is
that when I first designd to discharge him I sent for

him at St. *Alban's* and told him that I must have immediately the Mony that was in his Hands, which I think was about five hundred Pounds, which he allowd or more by his own knavish Accounts, and hee said I should have it as soon as hee could get it of the Tenants, but they had not paid him. Upon that I sent *Charles Myd.* to them, all round, and found it was a Lye, and that there was Nothing due from them, but little inconsiderable Things that were not worth naming, which had been owing many, many Yeares. Upon that I sent to *Cox* again, and then he begd that I would stay about a Month and hee would pay it all in to M^r. *Wilson*; and in that manner hee proceeded, lying and beging that wee would have Patience with him, and received the Rents a considerable Time, I think near two Years, after I said positively that hee should have no more to do with the Estate; and one Thing more is very remarkable, that when I was at *Aix-la-Chapelle* he write to the Duke of *Marlborough* to beg of him that hee would put a Stop to your Proceedings against him because it would ruin him, and that hee would be pleasd to excuse his Payment till he came into *England*, which the Duke of *Marlborough* thought so extravagant that hee made no Answer to his Petition, but let me write, as I did then to you, that you might take whatever Course the Law would allow of against so great a Knave. I don't like that *Myddleton* should give you new Troubles in his Accounts, for hee had very good and plain rules set him at my coming away, and hee is no Fool. I think a 184 Pounds a Year for the

Garden is a good deal, and I am sure more than it was when the D. of *Marl.* lived at St. *Alban's* himself, where to be sure they were kept more nicely then when they are sure one cant see them; and tho the Gardens may bee in good Order, tis certain that things are not don so often in a Garden that causes Expense when it is only keept so as it may bee made exact in a Fortnight's Time, as when the Master lives in it; and when that is the Case tis an ill Sign to have the Expense rather increase than lessen, but I see no Help for that at present if *Myd.* is not honest. I believe by what you say of the Mony paid allready to M^r. *Carter* that the Repairs have exceed very much what hee told you when you first gave yourself the trouble to employ him in that affair. I am glad that you are not in the Spleen, hoping that you see further then I, who you will find am very far, in my last, from buying Stocks; and indeed the Condition of my Country appears to me very deplorable, and exactly as M^r. *Steele* has describd it in the *Crisis*: 'the King of *France* is made strong, and all the Power of *England* put into such hands as will let no honest Man have quiet if they can help it, such as have so near compassd the Destruction of their Country, and by such vile Means *as it would be impious to make use of even for its Glory and Safty:*' those are M^r. *Steel's* words, but I protest I have had the same Thoughts a Thousand Times since I have seen all the wicked Proceedings of the Ministers.

I receive this minute the News of the *Queen's*

Relapse ; and if wee should be so unfortunate as to loose so good and so wise a Queen, I fear the Ministers have prepard themselves in her Illnesse to bring in the P. of *W*., in which case I must quote M^r. *Steel* again : ' Farewell Liberty, all *Europe* will soon be *French*.'

My humble Services and Thanks to M^r. *Boscawen* for his kind Remembrance of me.

No. 26.

To Mr. Jennens.

March the 14th, O. S. (1714).

Having the Opertunity of writing to you by a save hand, I chuse it rather than the Post, tho it will bee a few days longer upon the Way. I must, in the first place, thank you for your constant Goodnesse in our Concerns, and I am glad you had some Recompence for the Pains you took when you were last at St. *Alban's* in sleeping so well : tis certainly a very good Air, and I wish you would goe there oftener. In Three Hours, when the Road is dry, you may doe it with ease. I am sure dear M^rs. *Jennings* would like to goe with you and take Care of you, as I should like to doe Myself if it were in my Power. Lady *Sunderland* talks of sending her Children there some time this Sommer, but I hope that would not hinder you from going, for there is Room enough ; and if she should happen to bee there, you must needs be very wellcome to all my Family who are so good a Friend to us when wee are in a sort of an Exile ; but if you should have a mind to take the air when you happen to bee in the Spleen, and cant bear any Company, I beg of you to goe and see my Lodge in *Windsor Great Parke*, where you will find a very clean Place, and every thing that is convenient, and Nobody but a Hous Maid, the Gardener, and the Keepers, that will ride to fetch you anything you want at *Windsor*; and when the Court is not there, it is, of all the Places that ever I was in, the most agreeable to me; tho there is no Businesse, pray go and see it, for I love to hear that you have been in any Place that is mine; and I am confydent it will do you good, and if you send to Mr *Hodges*, who I have given the *best* Lodge in the Parke, he will ride about with you, and entertain you with shewing you a great many very pretty Places there abouts. I am intirely of your Mind, that it is not the D. of *Marl.'s* businesse to *fratch*. I love to have everything well don and in Order, but I cant help being angry sometimes when I find him so intolerably cheated as he has been allmost in all things of that kind; and I am glad you have given any Directions that will make the Farms in *Sandridge* in better Order, for that does me some credit, as well as the D. of *Marl.*, being my Estate; and I dare say it was not for want of cuting down Timber that it was not don before, for there were severall good Woods in that Mannor; and above Thirty Yeares agoe poor Mr *Guydott* orderd that there should bee non cut to sell, but honest *Cox* orderd it so that tho there never was any Timber cut to bring to Account, I dare say there is much less upon the Estate then there was when my Brother dyed, 35 Yeares agoe. When hee was taken into that Businesse he was not worth a Shilling, and I think wee have a very good right to have the Mony he owes us secured out of what he has cheated us of; but if there is not very great care taken, hee will give something in Security that is mortgaged before to somebody else, for I am apt to think that hee has over-purchasd himself. You ask me what you shall do with my small Summ that you expected to receive out of *Kent*, and I can answer nothing that is new: do whatever you will with it; I am sure I shall bee pleased and thankfull to you whatever the Event is. As to Publick Funds, you can judg much better than I if I were upon the Place: I can only say that I think wee never were so intirely in the Hands of Providence as now, for both Hous's of Parliament have given Assurances in their Addresses of all that the Ministers can desire. They say that all Men that have endeavourd the good of England are factious and rebellious, that the Q^n has taken care in her whole Reign to secure the Laws and Religion, notwithstanding that 12 Peers were made at one time to overturn them. In short I think what this Ministry has don is like to bee of much more ill consequence than what King *James* did that was deposd for it, and I need not say how much worse it is to those that are ruind by these Villians to raise their own Fortunes then if wee had sufferd by a Man that was still an Englishman, and would still have brought in Popery because hee was a weak man, and it was his Conscience. What these Men design nobody of common sense can doubt; but between the Men that are really and sincerely in the P. of *W.'s* interest, either out of Principle or for the Reward of their long Service in 25 Yeares Strugle with the Men that are so wretched as to bee bribed, you see they say all is safe under so wise and so good a Q^n. The Fleet will, if it is not allready, be put into the hands of those that will act for the P. of *W.*; and what Army is left will be disposed of in the same manner, so that whether the Q^n lives or dyes, whenever the Ministers and the French King can agree upon it I dont see what can prevent his coming. I have not the least doubt of anything in that matter; but whether they have brought the —— to consent to it in her own Life, or if hee is to stay till shee dyes, which hee may not now be easy with, since her health is said to bee very well establishd. After ruining most of the Allies and making the King of *France* so strong, I know nothing that could have prevented their Misfortunes but the Parliament having seen their danger; but tis very farr from that. I once had some small hopes that tho the rage of the Torys had hurt the Constitution for Fear of the Whiggs, who I believe have committed some faults, yet I thought there had been men of sense and fortunes considerable enough to have put the Government into honest hands; but that is over now, and I cant see that they will ever have another Opertunity. I expect that everything will grow worse and worse until they have brought the P. of *W.*, of

which, if you can doubt, I could convince you
thoroughly ; but tis not possible to write what I
know of the Matter, notwithstanding that there can
bee people so bad as to suspect the Protestant Succession in somebody's hands. This is all that I can
say to you : you must judg whether there is any
way to prevent these Mischiefs, which you may
depend upon it are designd, or if in case they are
compassd any Mony will bee secure in Public
Funds. On t'other side I don't know what to doe
with Mony abroad ; I have been told that it may
bee lent to the *Emp.* at 8 per cent. ; but when one
sees the Power of arbitrary Princes in these Countrys, and the Poverty of allmost all sorts of People, it
would make one fearfull of putting a great Summ
out of one's own Country if there were any hopes of
saving it there ; but for my little I have troubled
you too much. Once more doe what you think best ;
and if all the dreadful things happens that I expect,
and I outlive them, you will remember your Promise that I shall have one of your Cotages, but I
believe I must live even there in some disgise.

No. 27.

To Mr. Jennins.

(1714).

I have now the Favour of two Leters to thank
you for, and no more, tho you say in that of the
26th that I am three in your debt, besides that you
were writing, which makes me apprehensive that
two of your Leters are lost, for I am very certain

that I have now acknowledg'd all that ever I received from you ; and if you find it so, I hope you will have the goodnesse to repeat anything that may require an Answer. I am much oblig'd to you for your kindnesse in inquiring after my Friends, and sending me an Account of them. The Loss of my poor dear Child is indeed very terrible to me, tho I know there is a great many reasonable and true things to bee said upon such sad occasions, and that one ought to remember the Blessings which are yet left. That she is happyer I don't doubt then in such a World as this, where time generally passes away in trifling, in things that are tedious, and in many frightts for what may happen, which is yet worse. Something of this nature I believe wise people are sensible of, and that wee must all dye some time or other. I might add to this the deplorable Condition of our Country, and how near the prospect is of an entire ruin both to our Religion and Laws ; but all the Arguments that I can possibly think of cant hinder me from lamenting as long as I live the loss of what I had soe much reason to love as I had my dear Child, who had a perfect good mind and everything I could have wish'd in her ; but the impossibility of helping such Misfortunes, and length of Time, does certainly so far wear off the greatest Afflictions as to make one appear easy. This I know by experience, as well as that one has returns of many melancholly thoughts for the loss of those that I allow to bee in a much happyer condition than myself. My humble services to your best friend.

Aprill the 14th, O. S., *Wednesday.*

To Mr. Jennens.

Friday the 26th of *March*, O. S. (1714).

I have just now receivd the Favour of yours of
the 15th of this Month, in which you mention two
Leters of yours of the 3rd and 8th, which you say
you hope are come to me, and I don't remember
that I have had more than one of yours a great
While; but I know that I have answerd all that
ever I have receivd, and by that you will find if
any of yours have been lost, for I think all mine
that acknowledgd yours went by save Hands. But
I burn yours when answerd, and, as I have said
before, I forget the Dates. One of mine I know
you could not have rec^d when you wrote yours of
the 15th, and, I believe, it is yet on this side the
Watter. Wee have just now heard how Mr. *Steele*
has been used, which I think is far from a dishonour;
but as numbers must save or ruin *England*, and not
wise or honest Men, I give it over; there is Nothing
to bee expected that is good as long as the Mony
that the *P.* gives the Crown is made use of to corrupt all. sorts of people whos want of Worth, or
Necessity, makes it acceptable to them. As to my
Directions which you still seem to desire in my
private Affairs, I can say Nothing that is new. Tis
impossible for me to believe that Mony can be safe
in the publick Funds, or any where else long, after
the P. of *W.* is settl'd in *England*, or that the *Q^n*.
and Ministers design the Hous of *Hanover* should

succeed to the *Crown*, while they persecute all that
are in that Interest, and put the power into those
that are declar'd or known Friends to the P. of *W*.
There is other things that I know of that matter
which is not proper to write, but what appears to all
the World is sufficient; and I cannot believe such
Contradictions, tho' *Her Majesty* herself should every
Day give me new Assurances of it; but as I think
every Thing in *England* is very near being lost, I
have no great Opinion of any sincerity Abroad,
but Something I will have to keep me from quit
starving, which is as much as one could do in those
Countrys if one had all the Mony that the Ministers have given and taken to ruin *England*, once so
happy in Laws, and abounding in all Things that no
other Country enjoys.　　I am ever a faithfull Friend
and humble Servant to you and yours, more than I
can express.

No. 29.

To Mr. Jennens.

May the 7th, old stile (1714).

I have write to you so often in a few Days that
I should make many Apologys but that I am very
well assured of your goodnesse to me, and this is
occasioned by my having forgot to tell you that a
Person very knowing (who came to see my Hous)
has write me Word that the great Figures in the Hall
are well of the kind, but that the Battles, which are
small and at a great distance, are not strong enough
painted to be well seen.　　If this be rightly judged,

as I fear it is, I am sure you will doe what you can to have it mended in what is don as far as it can bee, and prevent the same Fault upon the Stair-cases, but they will bee seen much nearer than the Hall. I did not know till Doctor *Priest* told me, that I was obligd to you for the best Wine I have drunk since I left England. I shall not fail to drink your Health in it very heartily. You are good in every Thing to me, and I am more sensible of it than I can ever expresse. My Lord *Stanhope* dined with us To-day; hee is a very honest Man, I believe, and his good Sense, Wit, and Breeding makes him very agreeable. A Governour of some *French* Town would fain have persuaded him to goe to *B. Le D.*, and wondered that any Body could think the Person that lives there was not intended to bee our King.

No. 30.

To Mr. Jennens.

frankford, May 2d. N. S.

I have received the Favour of your Leter of the 30th *March*, and am glad to find by it that you have got rid of your Ague, and of Mr. *Aubrey.* I am confydent you may prevent the first from returning by taking the Barke, and the last, I will answer, shall never trouble you again upon my Account; and I flatter myself some Times, that I shall still live long enough in *England* to make him a looser by his Knavary. But I find he is a Man of Parts, which made him never mention one Word of the Alterations made after his Estimate was given in till I was at a good Distance from him, because tis certain there never was the least Thing changed after the Bargain was made, and my first Directions given, and hee knew I could have proved that; and for the Calash kept in 170$\frac{2}{3}$, I am more convincd than ever that there was no such Thing upon the D. of *M.'s* account, tho I am not much surprisd that a Man bread up fifteen Yeares by Mr. *Aubrey* should vouch for him any Falshood as that must bee; for Mr. *Reed,* who is now by me, asures me that he was perpetually in the Stables with Mr. *Bringfeild* a Year or two after the Time hee was supposd to have had this Calash, and that hee never saw any such Thing, but hee allways rid a-horseback as hee has don since; I mean Mr. *Reed,* so that tis certain there never was any such Calash, or else that it was don for Somebody else, who could not use the D. of *M.'s* Armes, and that part shews only the Wit of Mr. *Auberry* to make his Demand pass the better, and without that Contrivance it would have been difficult to make the Duke of *Marl.* pay for a Thing that was never orderd by him or me, nor mentiond till ten Years after he pretends to have kept it. And one Argument more there is to shew what a Rogue he is: at this time I have by me long Accounts of great Summs of Mony paid for the Duke of *Marl.* by Mr. *Bringfeild* every Year, and Acquittances at the bottome, which shews there was a Method, and that hee chargd all hee had paid or taken care of concerning the business in the Stables. But I have troubld you too much allready upon this

Subject, unless you were in any danger of making use
of Mr. *Auberry* yourself, and in that case you could not
bee too well prepeared against such a Man. I believe
in a little while I shall have a Leter from you with
an account of your Remarks at *St. Alban's*, the good
air of which place, I hope, will give you so much
Health as to reward you for the Pains and Trouble
you will take upon the D. of *M.'s* account, who I
am confydent will like whatever you are pleased to
doe in his affairs. Wee came to this place but upon
Saturday, and I have not yet been abroad. Tis what
I was allways told I should like, and that wee should
find all things that were good and convenient here ;
and by what I have seen in these Countrys, I doe
believe *frankford* is the best Town one can bee in
Abroad ; but indeed one must have sufferd a good
deal to make one find any Ease or Satisfaction by
being here ; and I am full of wonder every Day to
see Countrys that have been so long cevillised want
all the Conveniences of Life. We are now in one of
the best Hous's, I believe, in this Town, and yet
there is but one place that one can make a Fire in,
and the Weather is so cold that wee are half starvd,
for their manner is Stoves, which is intolerable and
makes my Head so uneasy that I cant bear it. In
short I have yet seen Nothing in all my Travells that
is worth giving you an account of but a Castle that
belongs to the Elector of *Treves*, which looks down
upon the *Rine* and the *Mosell*, two great Rivers
that mete, and there is several different Prospects
the most extraordinary and agreeable that ever I

saw. The *Elector* has a Hous at the bottom of this Rock where wee had the Honour to lye, and he would not bee satisfyd with any excuse from the D. of *Marl.*, but sent two Gentlemen, one after another, to desire him to come to his Hous, where he entertaind us very well, and there was an air of Greatnesse in every Thing about him. He came thro all his Rooms to mete the D. of *M.* at the topp of the Stairs that goes into his Court, and was extream civill, and eagerly so; and thro all the Places that wee have passd there has been Firing, and all the Markes of Respect to the D. of *M.* as if he had been the King of each place. And when one reflects that most of these Expressions come from Roman Catholicks, tis impossible to remember *England,* or at least the Governors of it, without Thoughts that I had best keep to Myself; but I have still so great an Interest in it that I often wish it were possible for our wise Cittyzens and country Gentlemen to travell and see with their own Eyes the sad effects of Popary and arbitrary Power.

No. 31.

To Mr. *Jennens.*

May the 13th, N.S. (1714.)

Last night I received the Favour of yours of the 16th of Aprill, for which I cant thank you enough; but it must needs tire you to bee perpetually repeating my Obligations to you, which can bee of no use to you, and therefore I will not trouble you with what I think upon that Subject, but put an end to

your Doubts concerning 9.   Whatever you think fit
to doe with that Figure, I shall allways bee pleasd
with, having an intire Confidence in you and 15 in
all Things, and I think the Arguement 15 had to
convince you to determine as you did concerning 9
was very just, only that I carry it a little further
than 15 did, for I think it looks as if 1, 3, 4, and 5
would be so usefull to 13 and 12 as to make 7 for
ever useless in *England.*   I am glad 7 has been so
well, and I believe that Person would not have gon
such lengths but with a Design to make all the
amends in their power for past Errors.   But there
are certainly some steps of that Figure that can't be
vindicated no more than the Peace, and therefore I
will let them sleep; and for 8, who is said to be a
little more cold than formerly in his old Opinions, I
believe that is Nothing more than being more
cautious than others, for I am sure he is too deeply
ingaged ever to change: it is so much harder for the
P. to do any Thing to secure the Publick after the
Address which I have seen from the *Lords* and
Commons of the 16th of Aprill than it was before,
that till I see it I can't flatter myself that any Thing
good can happen.   Some say they had commended
the Peace so much both in private and in publick
that they could not retract, and so to clear their
Reputations they voted what every Man, Woman,
and Child knows to bee false, since all the Facts were
made out so plain, and nobody could say one word
to justify the Approbation of such a Peace or vindicate the Ministry, and *England* must bee left in

the hands that have betrayd it, or they must contradict all they have voted this Sessions, which one
can't imagin possible for Men to do. I own I had
great hopes when the considerable Men ownd they
had been abusd with many Falshoods, and it had
been honourable and just to have resented such
Usage, and to have saved the Nation from it. But
since wee have received such great Advantages from
the good Councellors *Her Ma.* has had, and that
nothing has been don amiss, I cannot comprehend
what Good can bee hoped for from such a Majority,
and it looks to me as if there was no Difficulty but
that 1 can't comply with 13 till 11 comes to 1.
Every day the Letters are filld with honest Men
being turnd out of the Fleet and Army and known
Frenchmen put in their place. There is hardly Men
enough in *England* left to shutt the Gate against the
P. of *W.* and the King of *France* ; and in short, I
cant see the Possibility of turning *England* from
Ruin but an honest Ministry, and one of the Hous of
Hanover settled in *England*, neither of which, I
believe, will happen in my Life time. Pray give my
sincere kind Service to the she 15. There has been
such Arts used since the *Parliament* met to make
People believe that *Dunkirk* was at last to bee demolishd, that I will tell you what 'tis likely you
may not know, but what you may depend upon to
be true, that the 4th of *May*, N. S., Mr. *Hill* had a
Conference with Mons: *Le Blanc* about the demolishing immediately the great Sluces, which the
other flatly refused ; upon which the great Generall

was surprisd, and put him in Mind that he had told him upon Mr. *Armstrong's* last Return from *England* that he was ready to do it, and to obey all the Gov.^t Demands, and that there were severall Witnesses of it. But Monsr *Le Blanc* stuck to his Poynt, that hee never had received any Orders about the Sluces ; and more than that, that they were not in the Treaty to bee demolishd. The Men work two or three Days together to make a little Shew, and then leave off for ten Days together ; and in all this time there is but ten Coffers (I think that is the Name of them) taken up where they work at the Jettys, and there is in all Twelve Hundred. You may guess by this account of that one Perticular, how long it would bee doing if they were in earnest, but the Sluces is said to bee all that is of use to *England*, to destroy which he has declard hee will not do, and Mr. *Hill* sent his Secretary, Mr. *Forster*, to represent this to the Ministers, which shews hee is not in the Secret, for I dar say the Mins. would not have the Sluces destroyd no more than the King of *France*. There came two Battailions to *Dunkirk* the 4th of this Month, and they expect ten more.

No. 32.

To Mr. Jennens.

May the 16th, N. S. (1714).

Mr. *Priest* has told me Mr. *Cadogan's* thought about the Pannels of Wainscote in the Hall being painted, which I think will do very well, when I have Occasion (if ever that bee) to remove all my

Pictures to another Place; but I think 'tis much more likely that the D. of *M.* and I should bee removed into another World, and all our Hous's in the *Frenchmen's* power. Besides this melancholly Thought, there is a great deal of Painting to be don before 'tis necessary or reasonable to begin that; the two Staircases, which look ugly till they are finishd; and what I desire is to have them don first, and as soon as they can. My Bargain with Mr. *L'Guere* was, to give him five hundred Pounds for the Hall as I bespoke it down to the Pannills, and the two Staircases; but I am sure the Duke of *Marl.* will pay him as any good and reasonable Body will say hee deserves, if hee will doe it soon, and this you may be pleasd to read to him. You are in the right not to say more of the D. of *Marl.'s* Affairs at this distance. I believe it was never so little necessary to look into these matters as now, and when hee comes into *England* without your help it will all goe wrong again. I will trouble you no more by this Opertunity. My humble Services to dear Mrs. *Jenyns.* I hope your pretty Son is well.

No. 33.

To Mr. Jennens.

June the 6th, N. S. (1714).

I have troubled you so much since I heard from you that I should not doe it now, hoping all mine have been received; but I have a Mind to let you know that if Mr. *Degnar* and better Judges are of Opinion that the little Figures in the Hall does not

look too faint, that are at so great a Distance, and
don't upon that Account want any Alteration, there
is no Doubt that what is painted upon the Stairs,
which is so much nearer the Eye, will bee well, and
therefore in that I would not make any Alteration,
nor in the Hall, without the Approbation of the
skillful. You can expect no News from me but
concerning *Dunkirk*, which I believe you will be
weary of; and yet I wish I could send you a Plan
of it that is now before me, by which it appears very
plain that if it ever bee demolishd, that great
Advantage *England* expected in that is no more
then if one had made an Agreement (I think one
may say upon very valuable Considerations)
never to make use of that Port, and pretend
to make those Articles good by shutting up one
Door and opening another in the same Place: this
is just the case, and all People that understands this
Matter say, that what they are doing will bee a
much better Harbour than before to all intents and
purposes; and yet 'tis plain there is some civill Plott
still to save the old one, on account of the Expense
I suppose; for notwithstanding what Mr. *Bromly*
said in the *Hous of Commons* that the next Leter
would bring an account that the great Sluces were
destroyd, I know for certain, that the 28th of
May, this Stile, Mr. *Hill* sent to Mons.ʳ *Le Blanc*,
that if the Dames was not closed the next Day that
hee would send for the Keys of all the Sluces, and
that Nothing more should pass thro, to which
Mons.ʳ *Le B.* said, hee had received a Leter from

Court that the Sluces was to be keept open till the last Day of *June*, and desird to know if Mr. *Hill* had not received Orders conformable to that. Mr. *Hill*, looking upon this to bee a Scheam of Monsr. *Le B.*, he sent for the Keys the 29th. The next Morning Monsr. *Le B.* came to Mr. *Hill* and shewd him the Leter, that such a Negociation was on Foot for the Sluces to continue open for some Time longer, and while they remain open 'tis impossible for the Harbour to bee filld, and Mr. *Hill* sent his Aid-du-Camp express the 30th of *May* to Mr. *Prior* to know the meaning of this, that one Part contradicts Another, by which Way of proceeding there could bee no end of it. I have been thinking why Mr. *Hill* is so troublesome in this Affair, who would certainly bee very obedient to the Ministers, but I suppose 'tis because they won't give him Directions to press this Thing in case they should bee calld upon at any Time by the *Parliament* to see what they did in it. There is twenty Battaillions at *Dunkirk*, and 12 more expected, and the Irish Troops, both Horse and Foot, are going to those Frountiers.

I have write this Leter strangly, and I fear 'tis not intelligable.

No. 34.

To Mr. Jennens.

July the 2d., N. S. (1714).

I am now to thank you for the Favour of yours of the 15th and 22nd of May: the first I have had a good while, but the last I received but this Day, and I

am glad when I have a pretence of any Businesse to
write to you, being fearfull of troubling you when I
have nothing to say but one repetition of the Obligations that I have to you, which I believe you don't
chuse to hear of. Mr. *Jernas* doing his own Pictures, in the manner you say that are of value, is a
sure proof that he believes it a security ; but he is, I
think, a great Fopp, and conceited in many Things ;
and since you say you don't understand that matter,
I wish you would take an Opertunity of speaking
to my Oracle, Mr. *Moore*, for hee certainly has very
good Sense, and I think him very honest and understanding in many Trades besides his own ; and when
you have given yourself the trouble of hearing what
is to be said upon the securing these Pictures, I am
sure you will judg what is best to order, and do it.
I am very sorry for the occasion of your going into
the Country, tho if you had been well I think no
Place is so delightful, with such an addition as you
have in Family Comforts. I heartyly wish you may
enjoy them as long as 'tis possible ; but, indeed, you
never take great Care of your Health in order to
do so, and I fear you have not drunk Ass's Milk,
which I beg'd of you so earnestly to take. I am so
great a Physician that in these Countrys I am
followed like Dr. *Radley*, and I have lookd after my
Lord *Lonsdael's* Brother who has just got over that
cruell Disease of the Small-pox ; and without laughing,
I do believe I am better than any Physician even
in *England*, because I have been very well instructed, and I leave out all the knavish part of the

Profession, which gave my Patient so much Content that hee sent away his Doctor as soon as hee saw hee disputed about Trifles, and had no Medicines but mine that were good. I never saw Anybody fuller than this young Man was, but 'tis all over, and hee has been abroad to take the Air. I wish from my Heart your Son had escaped them as well, and I must needs give one harmlesse Advice which you may remember whenever hee has them, to put him on a Piece of fine Flannell three or four times double for a stay to his Cap, which I did to Mr. *Lowther* with so good success that he was not at all troubled with what is generally so very uneasy in the Small-pox, a sore Throat. I remember to have heard Dr. *Truer* say, upon twenty Advices of puting durty, stinking, troublesome things upon the Part to prevent a sore Throat, and that they might bee able to swallow tolerably, that it was all old Storys, and that Nothing was of any use, but to give Trouble, except great Warmth in that part, which made me think of Flanell ; and now I have begun this account I would fain have you follow my method upon any such Misfortune, that is, not to let your Son have any Strong Cordialls till the Disease has made the Discharge, and that the Face is falling. At that criticall Time what I gave poor Mr. *Guydott* is the very best thing in the World ; and while they are coming out, Nothing is so well as the Country way, a little Sack in Beer, Saffron, and Possett Drink, and the quieting Draft when they begin to want Sleep, which I made for about Eight Nights for this young Man, with as much Ease and Gravity as Mr. *Malthouse* could have don. I wish to hear you have taken a sufficient Security of *Cox*, which he is certainly very well able to give ; but hee will not doe it till hee is forced, you may depend upon it, but spin out the Time in hopes the Duke of *Marlborough* may come, and that he may tire him into Forgivenesse ; but I hope you will prevent that, for I have a natural avertion to all Rogues, and if the majority of my Countrymen had the same wee might yet bee the happyest and greatest Nation upon Earth. I have had so little Wit as to suffer myself to bee persuaded Sunday last to goe to *Mechline* to see a very extraordinary Procession, and I am not yet recovered—the Weather was so hott, and I was so extreemly tired. I never saw such numbers of People. They told me they came from severall Countrys, and that there were at least Thirty Thousand in the Town ; but I found Nothing so extraordinary in the Sight as that so many People could be pleased with such a rediculous Representation ; but they have a Folly for allmost every Day in the Year. The last in this Town that I saw was upon St. John's Day, and to do him Honour, a great many Children were dressed up in Lambes' Skins with little Bowles of Milk tyd before upon their Guirdles, which they eat as they walkd along. These Abuses in the Roman Catholick Religion makes one the more desirous to keep our own in the way it is as long as wee can, which can't bee expected to continue any Time after the P. of *W.*

is settled upon the Throne; and I cannot imagine how it can bee prevented, since 3 are so vile, 2 so false and wicked, 4 and 5 so corrupt, 6 so fearfull, and these People 15 mentions so foolish as to depend upon Chance rather then do any true and reasonable Thing for the good of themselves and Posterity. The poor old Electress, just before she dyd, sent me the Copys of the Queen's Leter to her and to the P. *E.*, and the Lord Treasurer's to her. They are all very extraordinary, and I think them so much worth your seeing that I would send them but that I believe you will see them without paying the Postage. 'Tis thought at Hannover the Queen's Leter touchd the old *El.* so much that it hastened her Death. She was certainly very desirous of having her Grandson in *England*, and write very moaningly to severall upon the subject of the Queen's Leters, which I will say no more of, concluding that you have read them. I had not the Copy of Her Majesty's to the *El.*, but I was asured that it was rather more furious against any of the Electors coming into *England* then those to the Electresse and young Prince.

SECTION THIRD.

HE Letters of the Duchess of Marlborough in this Section extend over a greater number of years than those of either of the former: namely, from 1714 to 1725,—three years after the death of the great Duke: an event, however, to which but little allusion is made. The close of the correspondence exhibits a strange and violent revulsion of feeling towards two of those who had hitherto been regarded in this correspondence as her most intimate and endeared friends,—her relative Mr. Jennens himself, to whom most of these Letters are addressed, and his near relative, Mr. Guidott. A dispute appears to have arisen with the latter respecting certain sums of money paid to him on the Duke's behalf, which the Duchess accused him of not having duly accounted for; and Mr. Jennens became involved in it, through his having been a party to some of the payments. A suit at law was the consequence, in the trial of which Mr. Jennens's evidence was most unsatisfactory to the Duchess; and her Grace's vituperations of them both present, it will be seen, a striking contrast to the courteous and complimentary terms in which she had been accustomed to speak of them. The incident is one that remarkably indicates and illustrates one of her 'ruling passions'—a passion which, she would lead one to believe, was 'strong in death.'

To Mrs. Jennens.

Windsor Lodge, Aug. the 10 (1714).

I have received the Favour of yours of the 31 *July* and that of the 6th of *August*, for which I give you a great many Thanks. I would have acknowledgd them at *London*, but I stayd so little there that I was in a great Hurry, and even here I have not Time to say what I ought to doe to you for so many obliging Friendships as I have received from you. *Friday* wee shall be at the *Bath*, where wee shall not stay above two or three Days, and about as long at *Woodstock*; after that wee goe to St. *Alban's*, from thence to *London*, when 'tis time for Ld *Marl.* to waite upon the *King.* I mentiond something to Mr. *Guydott* of hoping to see you at St. *Alban's*, but upon such Uncertainty I don't know whether it won't be best for you that I should have Patience till wee come to *London*; however, I will give you Notice when wee shall bee at St. *Alban's*, by a Leter from *Woodstock*, that you may doe what will bee more easy to yourself, which I ought to consider upon all Occasions more than my own Satisfaction. I was sorry to find when I came to Town that the businesse of *Cox* was not finishd, and upon it I desire the D. of *Marl.* to tell him when hee torments him at St. *Alban's*, that hee would do Nothing in it, but leave it to you and Mr. *G.*, who had been so kind as to take so much trouble upon his Account. This I found the D. of *Marlborough* much pleasd with,

and I was no less so Myself, for I should have been
very sorry that so much Pains as you have taken
should have been thrown away, or any part of it ;
and I hope after saying you would come to us to
any part of the World, you will still continue your
Friendship to the D. of *Marl.*, who, I believe, will
allways have as much need of it, in some Things, as
when hee was Abroad. I gave Mr. *Rea* Orders
to employ Mr. *Harris*, your Coach Maker, and I
had remembered you recommended an honest Man
at *Dover*, before I received your Leter. The D. of
Marlborough is your oblidged humble Servant, and
I am ever what I ought to bee to you and to dear
Mrs. *Jennens.*

No. 2.

To Mr. Jennens.

St. Alban's, Aug. the 23d, *Monday* Morning (1714).

Since my last to you from *Windsor* I have been
at the *Bath* and at *Woodstock*, and when I came to
this Place I was more tird than any of my Travels ;
and except when I was asleep, this is the first
Minute that I have been alone long enough to write
to you. I conclude you have seen the Duke of *Marlborough*, if you are in Town, as you said in your last
that you designd to bee. I don't yet know how
long I shall stay in this Place, but if you are well
and were at Liberty to come to us, I hope I need
not tell you how glad I should bee to see you and
dear Mrs. *Jennens*, if she can content herself with
such Conveanience as I can make in this poor

I

Habitation, which, however ordinary, I would not part with it for any that I have seen in all my Travells. Pardon my writing upon such a strange Peice of Paper, but I have nothing in Order or as it should bee yet, only my Heart, which will be allways yours, and you will be more wellcome to me than you can imagin, and yet you have Reason enough to expect every Thing that is possible from me as long as I live.

No. 3.

To Mr. Jennens.

Dec. (1714).

Reading your Leter over again, I cant find that there is the least Reason for any of those Reproaches in it, no more than for what surprisd me so much the other Day, only this, that the Duke of *Marlborough* did not present you to the *King*, which could proceed from nothing but Forgetfullnesse and the Hurry in which hee passed allmost every Day; but certainly it had been more like a Friend and a reasonable Man, if you had instead of being angry pittyd him, and said to him any Morning when you mett him so often, ' My Lord, tho I thought the Crowd so great at the *King's* first comming that it would signify nothing to bee presented then, I think it is Time now to put you in Mind of it.'

No. 4.

To Mr. Jennens.

Dec. 13, 1714.

I am too sincere to disown that I was more surprisd at the Violence of your Discourse the other Day than at any Thing that ever befell me in my whole Life; first, because I knew very well that I had never faild in any Thing to you; and next, that I had never perceivd before that you had such a Desire for any Place. I remember very well what I said to you at *St. Alban's*, which proceeded only from my great Inclination to serve you, had it been in the Duke of *Marlborough's* Power; but you seemd then so very indifferent in any Thing of that kind that you replyd you should like to do him any Serviss; but for yourself, you could spend fifteen hundred Pounds a Year and lay up a good Summ more; and I must own, considering your ill Health, and your Circumstances, I should have thought that you would have been a Footman as soon as a Groom of the Bedchamber; and when I said I thought you would not have accepted of that Employment, that Morning you were so very angry you answerd no more you would if it had been the same Trouble as in former Reigns, or to that purpose, by which it looks as if one of my great Faults was that I did not know your Mind without your telling it to me, nor believe that you had a great Desire to be in an Employment when you seemd by all your Discourse to have no Thought of it; and the first Moment that ever I found you had any Inclination for a Court Life was when you proposd two Things, which was chiefly, you said, for your Health and Pleasure—that was to have Hounds, and the Lodge in *Hampton Court Park*, both of which proved to be in the Duke of *Somersett* and the Earl of *Cardigan*, and I think I need not use many Words to persuade any Body that I had much rather you had any Thing than either of these Lords. This I say to remind you of all that passd between us on this Subject; at the same time I think there is very little need of my Excuses who cant bee supposd to have any Interest with any Body in the Court; and when I endeavoured to know your Mind at *St. Alban's* as to these Matters, if you had been otherwise inclind then you seemd to bee, I had no reason to hope that I could be of any great Use to you; but I was very desirous you should believe mee a good Servant to you, and very sensible of the Friendship you expressd·to the Duke of *Marlborough* and myself when wee were (as you termed it) in such Distress. At the same Time, if I know any Thing of myself, I would much rather have wanted any Assistance that you gave us, then that you should have been put to the least Inconvenience upon our Account; and this I can say very truely, that I am sure Nobody ever went two Steps to serve me but I would goe Ten to return it; tho I cant denie that People desire what they seem not to care for, nor can I get considerable Employments without any Interest when all the World are in a Strugle for them. And for the Duke of *Marlborough*, if hee has any Power it is still a Secret to me. I have seen no Effect of it yet. You seem to accuse me in this Leter that I refused to trouble you any further in the Affair of Lady *Russell*, which was certainly very naturall if you reflect upon those very extraordinary Things that you said to me some Days before ; and finding myself unable to return the Friendship I had received from you in the Manner you expected, it would have been most unreasonable in me to have trespassd further upon you. However, I find I must trouble you still in this Matter, for Lady *Russell's* Steward sends me Word that hee must have your Hand or Mr. *Guydott's* for a Year's Interest due the 29th *March*, 1714. I am very sorry for every Uneasynesse you have had or can have upon my Account, and am your most faithful humble Servant,

S. MARLBOROUGH.

No. 5.

To Mr. Jennens.

London, the 12th of *Aprill*, 1715.

I can't let the Post go without writing to you, since you could be so good as to say you should like to hear from me. But I have nothing in the World that is new to say to you that you will not hear in the publick Newspapers, except it is that Lord *Wharton* is given over. Doctor *Garth* sends me Word that he cant live till Night ; and to show what a publick Spirit I have, I do protest to you I should be very sorry for his Death, tho' he had been my mortal Enemy, having never in my whole Life seen so usefull a Man as hee was in the *Parliament*, and so constantly right in all Things that concernd the true Interests of *England*. I wish the last Ministry had been as honest in that, tho' they had been as villianous as they were to me and my Family. My Lord *Bullingbrook* was so imprudent, as soon as he came to *Paris* to send to desire that he might waite upon my Lord *Stair*, who excused the receiving that Visit as a Thing improper for him till hee had heard from *England*. If there is any true Happynesse in this World, I think you enjoy it now, in your own quiet Tent, good Sir, and a charming Woman that you have with a hopefull Son ; and if there is any Thing else that you desire, I heartyly wish that you may have it. I was told just now that one can have the Orders upon the Lottery of 1711 (which are the best) under one Pound odd among more than the Hundred and One melancholly tickit Things. They sell for about eight Pounds a Tickit.

No. 6.

To Mr. Jennens.

July the 8th, *London* (1715).

Mr. *Guidott* told me hee had sent you the Report of the Committee to the *Comons*, which I am sure will entertain you very much. I find many here are uneasy that the Articles are not yet carryd up to the *Lords*, and which is a sign that no Justice

will bee don upon any of the Traytors to their Country.   But I cant believe it possible that they would
have exposed them so much if they did not design
to goe further, and I rather believe the Delay proceeds from the great Desire of leaving Nothing
untold to the Publick in the Affair, and that the
Articles when they come on will answer the Length
of this that they have taken up.   There has been
a great Strugle this two or three Day about the
Duke of *Shrewsbury* going out and his *Majesty*
having a great mind to preserve him with his Staff.
But I hear that can't bee, and that if hee has not
allready given it up, it will soon be don, and that
both their Graces are to go into the Country in
order to prevent his being impeached.   I have had
a Leter very lately from Mr. *Diston* to give me
an Account of some Things concerning *Woodstock
Parke* in which I have given him Derections in what
I did understand, but hee mentions one Thing that
I must beg leave to trouble you in, about Mr.
Gregory's 112 Sheep—hee says 60 of them are now
remaining.   Mr. *D*. ask'd Mr. *G*. if hee had Orders
from the *Duke* to put in his Cattle into that Park,
upon which hee said hee had, for whatever hee
pleasd, but did not shew them, nor any Order from
you.   I ask'd Lord *Marlborough* what was the
Reason of such an Allowance and the Conditions of
it, but hee could remember Nothing of it but that
you had once spoke to him about it, and that hee
had, to bee sure, don any Thing which you thought
proper.   I desire, therefore, to know what the

Meaning of it is that Mr. *Distin* may have Orders in it, and that this Mr. *G.* may not abuse any Liberty that is thought fitt to give him. I wish to hear that you and dear Mrs. *Jennens* enjoy good Health, who am as much as I ought to bee your most faithfull humble Servant and Friend,

S. MARLBOROUGH.

Tuesday Morning.—The Duke of *Shrewsbury* gave up his Stick last Night very unwillingly.

No. 7.

To Mr. Jennens.

Sep. the 2d, *London* (1715).

I give you many Thanks for the Feavour of your kind Leter of the 21st of *Aug.*, and I am glad to find you are so sanguin upon the Death of the King of *France*, which I hope will make this Nation more safe and quiet then it has been since those Villians (who were his Friends) seized upon the Government; but still wee have Accounts from my Lord *Stair* that the Design goes on to invade us. The King of *France*, who was Guarantee for the *Hanover* Succession, was so honourable as to give the Value of fourscore thousand Pounds to begin this Design, and they write that it has stoppt from a Disappointment of Mony from *Spain* which they now think themselves sure of, and it is in our Mony about a hundred thousand Pounds; besides contributing which the *Pope* is to manage the Catholick Princes. My Lord *Marrs* puting himself at the Head of the People

that are up in the *Highlands* is a Sign hee has this
Intelligence, and hopes to succeed, and hee has been
allways reckond a Man of good Sense ; but I find
most of the People that I converse with think that
they can make Nothing of it, and that they have
slept their time. To bee sure, the Duke of *Ormond*
and such as his Grace presses them on, because they
cant bee well in a worse Condition than they are; but
since tis pritty sure the Man who is in the Place of the
King of *France* will not sustain them, I believe many
that promisd the *P.* to assist him will now be very
fearfull and cold ; but still if my Wish's could have
any Effect they should not bee try'd. You see by
this how often the Management of the Troops puts
us on a Precipice, and how often wee have been
saved by Miracles. I am quite weary of those that
say this Invasion is only an Invention—it is such as
without doubt wish the *Pr.* here—or are so silly
that 'tis Loss of Time to argue with them ; and whoever has a Tendernesse for the Men who have don
such Mischiefs to our Country I am confydent would
have acted the same Part had it been in their Way.
I allways understood that your Hous was so old that
you could do Nothing with it but pull it down, but
I am glad to find you were mistaken, for I have
never seen any new Hous so agreeable to me as
some old ones alterd, and I am sure that must
save a great deal of Mony, and I believe the true
Reason that Builders are so much against Alterations
is, because one can do that Oneself, and that Way is
much less in their Power. I am employd every

Morning at least four Hours in cutting out, and ordering Furniture for *Woodstock*. My next Bed will bee for the Room you chose, where I hope to see you often, and dear Mrs. *Jennens*, and I am sure you will never bee more wellcome to Anybody than to hers and your most faithfull humble Servant,

S. MARLBOROUGH.

When the *Highlanders* took up Armes they did not know that the King of *France* was dead.

No. 8.

Preston, Nov. the 13.

General *Wills* writes this Day that he came up with the Rebells the 12th and surrounded them. They are supposed to be 5000, being joined by most of the Roman Catholicks of the Country. They say there is in the Toune 15 Lords. It is reported that the Lord *Derwentwater* was killed when Mr. *Wills* made his Lodgement : he adds, that he hopes in a few Days to give the Duke of *Marlborough* a particular Account.

General *Wills* had but one Reg^t of Foot with him, but expected two more. This is the Substance of General *Wills's* Letter. Such a Resolution as his at the Beginning of these Troubles in all Probability would have set us at Ease long agoe, and saved the Nation the Expense of the Dutch Troops.

(*Tuesday* the 15th *Nov.* 1715.)

No. 9.

To Mr. Jennens.

Nov. 15th (1715).

Being in great Hast I have made the Account I
write of Mr. *Mills* to be coppyd to send to you. The
Pretender is saild *Wednesday* was Sennight to *Scotland*, and the Dutchess of *Ormond* told a Friend of
hers that she had been in great Trouble, but was
now at Ease, having received a Letter from her
Lord that he was safe in *Scotland*. One of my
Lord *Myddelton's* Sons is secured in the *Castle of
Ghent* by an odd Accident too long to write.
The Dutch Troops that are to come into *England*
are at *Harwich*, and the others at *Hull*. I am in a
great Hurry and can say no more but I think it will
goe well.

No. 10.

To Mr. Jennens.

The Account of the Robes for this five Years
comes but to £2312 a-Year, one Year with another,
including all the Sallarys and Payments to the
Officers thereof, which is between 4 and 5000 a-Year
less than it was in former Reigns, and about 2000
less than in King *William's*, without the Sallarys to
the Officers, who were then paid out of the Ex-
chequer, and if added to those Accounts will increase
them considerably. By these Accounts it appears
plainly that the Expense of the Robes has been much
less than in the former Reigns, tho they were then

when Cloaths were not near so expensive, and who ever would take the Trouble to look into the late Queen's Accounts would find that I have saved the Queen more then a hundred thousand Pound upon that Article since she came to the Crown. These are the first Accounts that were passd, and the Charge of the Coronation and all the Robes and Expense of Jewells were in them ; the Rest are passd and passing in the same Manner, and I have taken the same Care in the Accounts of the Privey Purse, which is subject to no Account, but there has been no Mony paid without an Acquittance, even to the Queen her self, and they have been kept with the same Exactnesse as if it had been the Mony of the Duke of *Newcastle.* It is a very new Thing to make Appologys for being a good Manager, but I am so unlucky, that People tell all Manner of Lyes of me, and therefore I must asure you that this vast Summ of Mony is not savd to the Queen by doing Anything that was wrong. Everybody has had what was fitt for them upon all Occasions, and the Differ-ance in the Accounts proceeds purely from the Care that I took that no Place should be sold of any kind, nor no Tradsman make any Present or give Mony as the old Custom was for being employ'd, nor so much as pay the least Poundage. The same Rules were observed in the Privey Purse, contrary to what had been practised by the Earl of *Portland,* and every Body before in the Office, and the Mony paid by a Goldsmith, to secure that no Mony should be given to Servants, which I thought wrong, and especially out of Pentions that were given for Charity, and all People were told that they were to pay Nothing, and that they had it from a Gold-smith for that Reason. (*Unfinished.*)

No. 11.

To Mr. *Jennens.*

Monday Night, *Windsor Parke.*

I am very much surprisd and troubled at the Occasion of your Leter, for I wish you might never have the least Uneasynesse, and I am sure this must bee a very great one. I am sure the Duke of *Marlborough* will do any Thing that is in his Power to serve you ; but for myself, there is Nobody in the World that is more insignificant, and Nobody, I believe, was ever better pleasd in being so then I am, unless upon any Occasion I want to serve a Friend. There is very few that I have Reason to call by that Name so much as yourself, to whom I shall ever bee a most faithfull, humble Servant, and to dear Mrs. *Jennens.*

S. MARLBOROUGH.

I design to be in Town upon Thursday.

No. 12.

To Mr. *Jennens.*

Jan. 3, 17, $\frac{16}{17}$, *London.*

I am so continually hurryd with Things of all kinds since I came to Town that my Head is allmost turnd, and I really don't know whether I have thankd you before for the Feavour of your last Leter; but if I have not, I am sure you will forgive me. The Duke of *Marlborough* said Yesterday that he found himself better every Day, which was more than the Doctor expected at this Time of Year, so I still hope that hee will be perfectly well when the warm Weather comes. One of my little Grand Children has had the Smallpox; I believe it is as bad a Sort as her poor Mother had, but I thank God she is out of Danger, and I think her Life is owing to her having had no Doctors, and in my persisting in not letting her Blood, which I think generally damps and lessens the Feaver which is natural to bring them out. Pray do me the Feavour to let me know who paid the Mony to the Man that paynted the Stairs of this Hous; hee tells me hee has received the three hundred and fifty Pounds—when I know the Certainty of it from you I will pay him the Rest. I hope you are well in your Health, and dear Mrs. *Jennens*, and that you both believe me as much as I ought to bee your most faithfull and most oblidged humble Servant,

S. MARLBOROUGH.

No. 13.

To Mrs. Jennens.

Sunday the 16th of *Aprill*, *Windsor Parke* (1717).

I give you many Thanks, dear Madame, for the Favour of your Letter. The Curtaine finishd is locked up at *St. James's* where I cant very easly send for it, and all I can desire of you now is that

you would bee so good as to see the Work before
you goe out of Town, that if you find it all clean
don, or any Thing else that you don't like, Mrs.
Bickmoor may be the more careful of it, and when
you come out of Suffolk I will be in Town to the
least Notice to your most faithfull humble Servant
and Friend,

S. MARLBOROUGH.

No. 14.

To Mr. Jennens.

Friday, May 17, *Windsor Lodge* (1717).

We came to this Place Yesterday, the Weather
being so bad that the Duke of *Marlborough* could
not go into the Gardens at *St. Alban's* ; hee was tired
with it in one Day, and hee fancyd he should be
better here ; but tis impossible to go out, and upon
my wishing for you and dear Mrs. *Jennens* hee said
you were to stay in Town the greatest Part of the
Summer, which I hope will make my Request more
easy than if you had Businesse in the Country. I
mean to make this Place your Home when the
Weather is warme and they all come to settle here ;
you may go as often as you please to *London*, and I
am sure this Air will do you good, and no Place can
be more agreeable than this is in the Three warme
Months. I am in hopes Mr. and Mrs. *Guidott* will
find some Time this Summer and make us a Visit ;
and tho the Hous is not large, I am confydent you
are all so good as to be contented with what there
is, and a very hearty Wellcome. You shall ride and

walk and be alike free as if you were at Home; if I could think of any Thing more to tempt you I should be glad to say it, for I think the Duke of *Marlborough* will be much the better for Company sometimes, and I hope I need not say much to persuade you that yours is allways very acceptable to your most faithfull and most humble Servant,

S. MARLBOROUGH.

I hope wee shall be soon in Town, but I write this now to beg of you that you will order your Affairs so as to give us this Satisfaction.

No. 15.

To Mr. Jennèns.

Windsor Parke, Monday the 29th *Sept.* (1717).

Wherever this Leter finds you I hope you will not proceed in reading it till you happen to be at Leisure, for I forsee it will bee a very long one, and you may take your own Time for it. I give you many Thanks for both your Leters, and for the great Care you took of the Box and Picture. The little one of me, I hoped Mrs. *Jennens* would weare sometimes to put her in mind of me, and when we mete in Town I must desire the exact Bignesse of her Finger to sett it in a Ring. The Duke of *Marlborough*, I thank God, is at least as well as hee was, notwithstanding that the Weather is not so good. Hee does not think of leaving this Place yet, and when hee does so I am sure he will want the Advantage of taking the Air so easly as hee does here, and bee weary of

London. I am sorry to find you are not so well as
you were, but I am glad you are so good to us as to
take what most People would have thought a
Trouble. You mistook in thinking my Help was
desir'd in this last Illnesse, which was truely no more
than I will give you an exact Relation of. The
great Lady was taken ill upon this Day Sennight,
of a sore Throat and Thrush ; the Husband is
certainly very kind to her and good natur'd, I
believe ; but very young, and ignorant as to any
Thing of Distempers ; and 'tis plain by what I saw
when I came that Doctor *Mead* had frightend him
out of his Witts, in order, I suppose, to bee paid the
better, and to value his great Skille ; but I never
heard a Word of her Illnesse till Friday Morning at
8 o'Clock, when a Messinger came to acquaint me
that the Lady was so ill that the Lord could not
write, and the Man told my Servant that hee
believ'd she could not live an Hour, and look'd
extremely concern'd and frightend. 'Tis certain
that when that Messinger came they gave her over ;
and I am apt to think by all the Manner of it that
Somebody there thought it not decent to let her dye
without giving a Grandfather and Mother some
Account of it, that were but Twelve Mile off, and
from whom she had had her Portion ; for when I
call'd for my Coach to go to her, before the Duke's
Servant, hee seem'd very uneasy at that, and desir'd
me not to go by any Means, saying that in a few
Hours she would bee better or worse, and that it
was better for me to send a Servant back with him

who might bring me Word how she was, and Servants generally knowing the Minds in that sort of Matters of their Masters or Mistresses (if hee was not instructed to hinder my coming), I concluded that hee knew they would rather have my Room then my Company; however, as I could not but think she was in great Danger of her Life, I was resolved I would not be discouragd by any Proceedings of theirs to doe what I could to save her, or at least to bee satisfyd there was no Help if she dyd, and I got into my Charriot and was at *Claremont* in less than Two Hours. When I came to the Door Mr. *Pelham* met me, and I was so careful of making no Disturbance at such a Time that I askd him to let me see Doctor *Sloan* without seeing Doctor *Mead*, which I believe you will think was right, after his bruital Behavior in Lord *Spencer's* Illnesse. To this hee answerd very readyly that I should not see him, and lookd as if hee was glad of that Request, for I am confydent it was settled before I came in that I should neither see him nor the Dutchess of *Newcastle*, for hee carryd me into a Room where the Duke was, Doctor *Sloan* and Mrs. *Pelham*. The Duke lookd very grave and wise, as if there was great Danger, and I must needs own that the Duke shewed great Tendernesse and Passion, and the whole Appearance was so dismall that I fell down and cryd with them, by which I think there is such a Thing as natural Affection in some People. Mrs. *Pelham* was in Teares to, but as soon as I could speak, upon asking Questions I found that she had

no Heat in her Flesh, that Something had broak
in her Throat, that her Hands were moist, and that
she had Sweat; that she had been a little light
headed by Fitts, which no doubt was her want of
Sleep, because it was quit gon upon a Glister working very well. All this composed me very much,
for I could not easyly believe that one of seventeen
could dye of such a Distemper, when she had been
blooded and the right Things applyd to her; and
after setting allmost an Hour in this Room, speaking to every Body that came from the Dutchess,
to make them all easy, I said to the Duke I will not
desire to see her for Fear of troubling her; but for
God's sake, my Lord, do you goe into her, and don't
let me constrain you, which hee would not doe by
any Means, giving it this civill Turn, that hee did
not goe to her for Fear of making her talk, which
would bee a Prejudice to her; so I offerd to go away
with a great many good Wishes for her Recovery,
from which, out of great Civillity, hee desired me to
stay a little; and I answered that I could stay for
ever if I could do any Good, and sett down again;
but in some Time I took my Leave without seeing
her, or being asked to do it, and I went away very
contentedly, for I saw plainly by Mr. *Brown* the
Surgon's Face, who is very able and honest, that
hee had no Thought like what the Doctors had
represented. I am sure you have often heard of my
Passions and Assautments, but I fancy you will think
that I governed them upon this Occasion, if I have
such Things, as well as wise People doe; at least,

that I have had the Happynesse to know. I left a
Servant to bring me Word how she was, as soon as
any Change happend, and several Messages and
Leters has passed between me, Doctor *Sloan*, and Mr.
Pelham, and Yesterday I had a very good One from
the Duke of *Newcastle* in which hee says as follows :
that hee thanks me for my Kindnesse and Advice, which
hee shall never forget as long as hee lives, and is sure
that the Dutchess of New. will bee exceedingly sensible of
it, and will make all Manner of Returns of Gratitude
and Duty ; but as these Professions have been made
before in the Midst of all the ill Behaviour imaginable, I must conclude that both shee and hee are
persuaded that she has performed well, and I expect
no Change in her, nor desire non, being of the
Opinion that if the Heart is not right Nobody can
make it so by any Arguements, and I wish I had no
greater Uneasynesse then I shall have upon her
Account, though I was very sorry when I thought
she would dye, and wish she may live to her own
Satisfaction. I will now venture to trouble you with
another Account concerning Mr. *Diston* ; I told you
my Opinion of him before I left *Woodstock*, when I
was convincd, after hee was put in Possession of
that Businesse, that hee intended, like Mr. *Reeves*, to
turn the Advantage of it all to his own Account,
and every Thing helps to confirm me yet more in
that Opinion. I don't know whether hee has heard
that hee is not to have the Lodge, as hee had the
Folly to request ; but hee is allarmed, I am sure, at
the Directions I wrote concerning the taking no more

Cattle into the Parke, and he has write me a long
Leter, in which hee would value himself by making
me think hee would take great Care to prevent the
Abuses that have been in the Harriottes due to the
Duke of *Marl.*: hee writes that hee spoake to you
about them, and that you said you thought hee
should do in that Matter for the D. of *Marl.* as other
Men of Quallity did in the same Neighbourhood,
which was certainly very right ; but hee never mentiond these Harriottes to me, tho I had so much
Time with him, tho now hee writes that hee had
compounded for Four Cows, for which hee took
Nine Pounds Ten Shillings. I believe that is very
easy; at least I doubt, when I come to buy Cows I
shall not find that they are bought so cheap for me.
In this Leter hee tells me one Mr. *Gregory* owes
for Four Harriottes, which if the Duke of *Marl.*
insists to take but Fourty Pounds for, hee uses him
very kindly; but hee has never yet offerd him more
than Twelve Pounds for these Four Harriottes, tho
hee showd him plainly the Injustice and Unreason-
ablenesse of it. I dont know if this *Gregory* is
the same Person that the Duke of *Marl.* has
employd about his Estates in *Oxfordshire*, but hee
gives but an ill Description of him ; and if it bee that
Man, I believe it is likely to be but too true, for I
think his Accounts to Mr. *Guydott* are very extravagant ; but I fancy if it is the same Person Mr. *Diston*
says out of Apprehensions, that hee is to manage for
me, more than out of any true Honesty to the
Duke of *Marlborough*. I expect every Day the

Man that I intend shall look after all the wild People that the Duke of *Marl.* has aroused, and I think to send him first to *Woodstock*, and then round to all the Estates ; and if hee should not bee so good and honest as I am told hee is, and as one would be-speak a Man for that Employment to be, yet he will be a great Check upon the Bailys, and they will be some upon him, who they will hate for taking the Businesse cheifly out of their Hands. The D. of *M.* came into me just now and askd me what you said about the Lodge, upon which I told him all your fine Speeches at first, and how it ended ; and upon this Subject Mrs.' *Jennens* came into the Discourse at last, and I found hee was so much pleasd with her that if hee returns I believe you must have an Eye upon her ; but I am resolved to love her, how-ever hee behaves. I am now so great a Philosopher that I fancy few Things will disturb mee after what I have passd thro in my unhappy Life.

I forgot to say that I dont remember any Thing, at least considerable, in Mr. *Reeves's* Accounts upon the Head of Harriottes. The Businesse between him and Mr. *Beeston* altogether, as I remember, never exceeded much Twenty Pounds a Year, and now it is come out that Forty Pounds is due from one Man, and Nine Pounds Ten Shillings taken for Four Cows, and hee talks of going round the Hun-dred as if there were still great Things to be receivd.

The Doctors behavd just as I fortold they would do : when I came Home upon *Friday*, the first Leter was that they would not say the Dutchess was out of

Danger, but in a very fair Way; this was Yesterday Morning, and the next Day all was safe, for after such great Alarm you must think that even their Skill could not secure her all at once.

To Mr. *Jennens*.

Oct. 20, 1718, *Windsor Lodge.*

I have now two of your Leters to thank you for, and I should have acknowledgd that from *Suffolk* sooner but that you talkd then of coming soon to Town. The *Dean* would give you an Account of the D. of *Marl.*, who, I think, is better then when you saw him. Notwithstanding the Winter is come, hee has sett no Time for leaving this Place, but says hee will continue here as long as hee can, and as long as hee likes it, and finds any good by going out to take the Air. I shall bee better pleasd with being here then in *London*; but at this Time of Year wee cant stay long, and the Duke of *Marlborough's* Humour allways was to remove of a suden without giving much Warning; and I am glad that you and dear Mrs. *Jennens* are come to Town, that wee may bee sure of the Satisfaction of finding you there. I believe the *Captain* is gon long since that was to carry the Box to Mr. *Gore*, so that it will bee Time enough for me to have it when I come to Town, for I have no Curiosity, and if Mrs. *Jennens* likes it, I believe Mr. *Gore* will find no Fault with it; but I will send Mony to pay for the Box and Picture if you will do me the Feavour to let

me know what they come to. I don't remember
any Thing of the *Spectator* you mention, but I have
had so much Experience of you and of dear Mrs.
Jennens, that without more Complements I am desirous to take you both for better for worse ; and I
hope you will believe that I shall allways bee your
faithfull humble Servant, tho very insignificant.

No. 17.

To Mr. *Jennens.*

Woodstock, Aug. 22, 1721.

I have had so much Businesse that I have not
yet had Time to goe to your Lodge but one Night
when it was allmost darke and I could see Nothing.
But it look'd very melancholly, and I know it will
never bee so agreeable as when Mrs. *Jennens* was
Mistresse of it. But I think it is allways right to
submit to what is most for the Service of our
Friends. If there is any Mistake in the inclos'd
Note for the Mony, I must clear myself from that
by laying the Fault upon you, for what I desird was
that you would make up the whole Account, but as
you did not I was forc'd to get *Hodges* to do it. I
find Mrs. *Jennens* has left me a Present of Malt
Drink. I have tasted last Night the three Sorts.
Non of them are bitter, but the Ale and Strong
Beer I doubt will never be fine, unless she can
derect any Way to make it so ; because they tell me
it has been brewd two Yeares ; tho' it is not fine,
but the Beer is extreamly good. I have non of my
own that is so, which I think is very strange, if it

bee true what they tell me, that the same Man that brewd hers has brewd mine. I have given great Charge that not a Bottle of this small Beer shall bee drunk but at my Table, which will put me in Mind of drinking her Health often.

I am your most faithfull humble Servant,

S. MARLBOROUGH.

No. 18.

To Mrs. Jennens.

Munday.

You have been very kind and very good, dear Mrs. *Jennens*, since my great Misfortune* in offering to come to me. I own that I have seen several of my Acquaintance which, as it was orderd, I thought I could not well avoid, but I had been much more easy if I had seen Nobody. I conclude you are in Town, and if you are I believe this fine Weather will bee of some Advantage to you to remove into the Country; and if you will come to *Windsor Lodge* you shall bee as welcome to me as I can make you, who am allways your most faithfull humble Servant,

S. MARLBOROUGH.

My humble Services to Mr. *Jennens*. I conclude what I say to you is the same to him, so I will not trouble him with a Leter.

* [The death of the Duke of Marlborough.—ED.]

No. 19.

To Mr. *Jennens*.

August 29, *Windsor lodge.*

I find by the Favour of yours of Yesterday that you cannot aford me more than one Day at this Lodge, and therefore I send this to say that to make it more easy to your Horses, if you will please to say when you will come I will send mine to meet you at *Hounslow*. I should have offerd this before but that I hoped to have had you and Mrs. *Jennens* longer, whos Company is allways very wellcome to your most faithfull

Humble Servant,
S. MARLBOROUGH.

No. 20.

To Mrs. *Jennens*.

Sept. the first, 1722.

As soon as you were gon, dear Mrs. *Jennens*, I sett down to thank you for your kind Nettin, and I hope this Keeper will give me the Satisfaction of leting me know that you got safe Home. Since Mr. *Jennens* said that hee did not goe out of Town till the Middle of the Week, I beg of him that hee will read this long Paper to you before hee goes. If you knew what I have sufferd in having such vile Things said of me, you would not wonder at my collecting what I have don in my own Vindication, and I dare call God Allmighty to witnesse that 'tis all true if I were to dye this Moment. And

some Things at the end of this Account which I
doubted of, I am now certain is true likewise. I
mean as to what these Ladys reported of me when
they went to *London.* I believe when you come
to the End of this melancholly Paper you will be
amazed that it should bee possible for human Creatures to torment and grieve such a Father and
Mother for so many Yeares without considering
how much had been don, and how little was expected from them. I have all the Vouchers by me
of this Account, but I don't send them, because I
think you will not doubt of the Truth, and acci-
dently might happen to have them lost, which I
should be very sorry for, because they shall be found
in my Cabinet when I am dead with this Account.
When Mr. *Jennens* has read this Account, I desire
hee will seal them up, and give them with his own
Hand to my Porter, Edward *Seagrave,* at *Marlborough Hous.* I am most faithfully yours,

S. MARLBOROUGH.

No. 21.

To Mr. Jennens.

Sept. the 6, 1722.

I give you and dear Mrs. *Jennens* a great many
Thanks for the Patience you both had in reading
over the long Paper, and for your kind Expressions
to me. I can desire no more than that you will
vindicate me from such vile Aspertions, for if there
had been a Possibility of a Reconcilement (after
what has lately happend) I would never have

exposd such Crimes in my Children ; but as it is, I think I should not neglect my own Character so much as to bee thought in the World the worst of Women, when I know I have allways endeavoured all the Good that was possible to my Family; and I believe that whoever has a Love to Truth, Humanity, or Honour, when they know the Story, they will justify me. I do asure you that the whole Account is as true as that which you have been a Witnesse to yourself; tho I own when I was collecting the Whole together, and making the Leters be copied into it, I thought as you did, that it was incredable, and that it sounded like the Story of *Robinson Crusoe.* I hope now there will bee a great deal of dry good Weather for your Journey into the Country, where I wish you and Mrs. *Jennens* all Happynesse, and am to you both a very faithfull humble Servant,

S. MARLBOROUGH.

No. 22.

To Mr. Jennens.

Sep. 10, 1722.

You will think there is to bee no End of the Trouble of my Leters, but there being new Matter in yours I can't resist giving you an Account of what I know of that Story ; and if I have committed any Fault to that great and wise Lady, 'tis the First in fourty one Yeares. I will begin with the last Part of what you have heard. I never saw this Man taken out of Prison in my Life, nor is he taken into my

Family, but there is more Ground for this than there
has ever been for any Thing that has been reported
of me.   The Fact is as follows, and is certainly the
exact Truth.   Many Yeares agoe a Friend of my
Lady *Godolphin* recommended a Boy to her for a
Page, whos Family had once three thousand Pounds
a Year, but all the Child's Relations were dead, and
he was reduc'd to Want of Bread.   L^{dy} *Go.* took this
Boy and put him to learn of a Master that teaches
my Children to read and write, and cast Accounts :
his name is *Hothard*.   After that she got him some
little Place in the Government, and her Steward often
employd him to feetch Mony from Mr. *Edwards*.
About two Yeares agoe the Steward sent him for a
Hundred Pounds, but happend to fall sick before
hee came with it and continued so six Weeks, and
never call'd for the Mony.   This young Man's Salary
from the Government was so ill paid that hee was
very much in Debt for Cloaths and Subsistance ; and
being press'd for his Debts, he brook this Hundred
Pound Bag, hoping hee should get the Mony due to
him, and make it up ; but before hee could get it
the Steward call'd for the Mony, and the young Man
out of Shame and Fear ran away and went out of
England, but is come back, not being able, I suppose, to get Bread Abroad.   As soon as hee came
hee went to this Steward hoping that hee would have
Mercy upon him till hee could pay the Mony, but
instead of that hee put him into Prison for it, and
said it was by his Lady's Order, and I dar say his
Lord knew Nothing of it.   The Writing Master

hearing of the misserable Condition that this Youth was in, and loving him, for hee said hee was the best Servant that ever hee had in his Life, went to see him and gave him Mony for his present Support; but the Debt was too much for him to pay, and Mr. *Cudworth* applyd to me for it. I thought it was too much with the Fees and Cloathing to give to one that I never saw, and advised that hee should apply to my La. *Go.*, which hee did in vain; and upon severall Applications to me, in about three Months I sent one to the Prison to give him Something to keep him from starving, who lately gave mee an Account that hee was in the most miserable Condition that hee had ever seen any Body, with a Shirt as black as a Hood, his Cloaths but half enough to cover him, and all full of Lice. Upon this I orderd his Debt to bee paid, and cloathd him, and I was told that his old Master would give him Businesse when hee was out of Prison, and support him. This is all that I know or have don in this Matter. If my La. *Go.* had been only an Acquaintance of mine that had lived civilly with me, I should not have don this without speaking to her of it, and I think it is a known Rule that Nobody takes the Servants of those that live but decently with, before they first inquird what they went away for, and if it bee not disagreeable to that Friend or Acquaintance to take them. But I never thought of taking this Man; and if I had, my Daughter has shewn me that that Ceremony is needless between her and me, since she has taken my Servants that were put away for

Crimes that they deservd to be hang'd for. But that does not trouble me, for I have severall yet that are only good for Nothing, and I intend to provide for them the same Way. I think the World is much inclind to find Fault with me, since this is imputed to me as a wrong Thing. All I can say is, that *Cudworth* is not the first Person that I have taken out of Prison; and if my Daughter had not put him in, I should have don the same Thing, and let the foolish and malicious part of the World say what they will, I do think this Man was a great Object of Compassion, and it was no Injury to the great Lady, since the Debt was what she desir'd, tho I cannot help observing at the same Time, that she has Starts of giving a hundred Guineas to a very low Poet that will tell her that she is what she must know she is not, which I think so great a Weaknesse that I had rather give Mony not to have such Verses made publick. But as to the cruell part of this unfortunate young Man, I am sure if the poor Duke of *Marlborough* would have put People into Prison, hee might have fill'd one with Servants for Crimes that were much worse than *Cudworth's* ; but in his Life hee never did more than put them away, and often when they were gon he gave them Something to keep them from robing. Since you are in the Countery I hope this long Leter will not make you repent the telling me of this Report ; for tho it is not possible to prevent Lyes being spread, and wrong Twist given to every Thing, it is some Satisfaction to tell the Truth upon such Occasions, and that is what I will allways stick to, whether I have don well or ill; and if one has judged ffoolishly, I think it is never mended by disowning of it. I am glad to see the Weather so good for your sake and dear Mrs. *Jennens'*, who am your most faithfull and most

humble Servant,

S. MARLBOROUGH.

No. 23.

To Mrs. Jennens.

Friday at one.

I send your Pendance and Buckle because I think you will not care to carry them Home at Night, but the Knott upon the Hatt is so pretty that I beg leave to keep it as it is a Day longer, because I will shew my Children to one or two of my Friends drest as they were Yesterday.

When I made my Compliments today to my Lady *Portland*, I thought it proper to say Something of what had happend at the Door with the Porter; and I send you her Answer, because I think it is reasonable and civill. I hope you are well and Mr. *Jennens*. I will not ask you to dine here unlesse you happen to like it, tho' I have Nobody but La. *Ann* and La. *Charlott*, for the little Ones dine abroad. If you come, why should you not bring *Dolabella* with you?

No. 24.

To Mrs. Jennens.

Dear Mrs. *Jennens*,—I have lookd upon this Damask by Day Light. The Pattern is not so large as she stated, but hee has kept it so ill that it looks full as old as what I have, which is better than if it were a fine fresh Damask. But I think it is a good Argument to him to sell it cheap; for tho I like it very much for this Use, I would not buy it for any other. But don't part with it, for I would have the whole Piece upon any Terms that you can get it.

I shall want a vast Number of Feather Beds and Quilts. I wish you would take this Opertunity to know the Prices of all such Things as will be wanted in that wild unmercifull Hous, for the Man you go to is famous for low Prices. I would have some of the Feather Beds Swansdown, all good and sweet Feathers, even for the Servants. I am not in Hast for any Thing you are so good as to do for me.

No. 25.

To Mrs. Jennens.

Sunday the 25th of *No.* 1722, *Windsor Parke.*

I reckon dear Mrs. *Jennens* has been so happy ever since her Son came Home that she did not care to bee troubled with any Body. I wish hee and you may live long to enjoy one another, and that hee may ever make you Returns suitable to the true Care and Tendernesse which you have ever had for him ; and if this happens I am sure I need not desire any Thing more for you, for I believe good Children are the greatest Blessing that God can give to a good Parent.   Now I have made my Prayer, I will begin the Businesse of my Leter, which is, to desire when you are at Leisure to see if there is any Indian Calicoes, or Chinna Tufatys, or Damasks deep blue to bee had for Furniture.   I am not in want of any, but the Act coming very near forbiding the Use of them, I fancy the Treadespeople will bee glad to sell them now upon easy Termes.   If you see any Thing that you like, and will do me the Favour to buy it for me, I am sure I shall like your Fancy, and I can make them up by Christmasse, having Nothing to do but to amuse myself with such Things.   I was sorry to see in the Newspapers that a hundred thousand Pounds was to be raised upon the Roman Catholicks.   I wish it may be turnd to a good Use ; but I own I think those People that take Oaths to the Government and pretend to be of the Religion of the Country deserve to suffer more when they act against the Laws.   All that I can say for this Hardship to People that act upon what is natural in them is, that if they were in Power, I believe they would make us suffer a great deal more. I am ever yours, dear Mrs. *Jennens,*

S. MARLBOROUGH.

My humble Service to Mr. *Jennens* and to your Son.   If you like Doe Venison, I will order some from *Woodstock*, and to Mr. and Mrs. *Guidott* if they

care for it. The Officers demand so much more
from this Parke than they did in the *Queen's* Time,
that in Doe Season I am forcd to send for my own
from *Woodstock*, which in cold Weather comes as
well to *London* as from *Windsor*, and I believe the
Venison is better.

No. 26.

To Mrs. Jennens.

Wednesday.

As busy as you see me every Day, I am in great
Distress at this Time, having no Night Close but
Rags, and having no Help from any Body but my dear
Daughter, nor Comfort but from her and her good
Children. I send you these Things, and desire four
Suits may be made just as the last were. The Pattrons are inclos'd, and pray desire the Woman to
put the Lace on as full as it will require, because I
am told that when they are wash'd the Lace will
shrink and not look well if that is not allow'd for.
I would have the Woman wash the Cambrick before
she setts on the Lace. If Mr. *Jennens* and you are
not engag'd, I shall be glad you will dine with me
as late as you will, and I hope you will mete your
Children.

No. 27.

To Mr. Jennens.

August 13, 1723.

I will begin this Letter with begging your
Pardon for being so disagreeable last Night in not
minding my Play, for which after you were gone I

was punishd with losing my own Mony; but that makes not amends to you. The Sight of the enclos'd Bill will naturally make you a little peevish, therefore I make Haste to tell you that I don't trouble you in it with the least Design of desiring that you should do any Thing in it, but purely to vindicate myself to you, that you may not think that I have done any Thing that is wrong; for I know Mr. *Harris* will complain to you, and not be fair in giving the Account. The Deduction upon the Outside of the Bill is really no Abatement, for he has put down £5 for a slight Glass that was broke by the Servants in a Coach which he lent for them. The six Pounds ought not to have been charg'd at all, Mr. *Reed* having protested to me that Mr. *Harris* told him when he wanted a Coach for the Servants to carry them to *Windsor*, that he had one which was of no Use to him, and that he would have Nothing for it. When he wanted it he would send for it, which he did not do (as he says) in 12 Weeks, and the Children did make Use of it Sometimes to carry them to *Foubert's*, but it was not at all necessary, because there was another Coach and Charriot in Town, and it was Mr. *Harris's* own Offer, which was no very great Thing considering how much Mony he has taken of my Family. This reasonable Reduction reduces his Bill to £102 3s. 6d., and I offerd him Yesterday a Bank Bill of £100 for it, notwithstanding that I have computed in this Bill that about 36 or 37 Pounds of it is for keeping only one Coach, not very much used since *August* 1722;

and formerly *Hodges* agreed with a Man for £15 a Year (by the Year) for doing that Business. There is another Thing which does not appear in this Bill that I have passd over in the Bill to ye Executors, which is that he has had 48 Yards of Black Cloath to line and cover the Mourning Coach and six for Harness, which is enough to cover my Garden; and I have upon Enquiry found that several Coach Makers have offerd to do it with 35 Yards, which I dare say is more than can be put on of Cloath of that Breadth. I am sure you will think that Mr. *Harris* is very much in the Wrong to have made any Dispute upon so very small an Abatement in such a Bill, and that is all I desire, for it is all one to me whether he takes his Mony now or a Year hence, since I will never give him more; for tho one squanders away much greater Sums every Day, it is disagreeable to be so much imposed upon.

You may have a Party at Play Tonight if you like, for there will be two Tables, and you may chuse to be with two that wont be always asking who plays the Game and what is Trumps. I hope dear Mrs. *Jennens* is better Today. I am hers and your most faithfull

Humble Servant,

S. MARLBOROUGH.

No. 28.

To Mr. *Jennens.*

July 17, 1725, *London.*

I have been kept a great while in Town longer than I wishd upon extraordinary Businesse, and now have a great Addition to it by the Executors' Suit with Mr. *Guidott.* For notwithstanding his godly Professions to them, laying his Hand upon his Heart, and assuring them y.ᵗ he would never stand upon Privilege, yet he has stood upon Privilege, and till some Days after the *Parliament* rise last Sessions, when he would have been sequesterd if he had not put in his Answer. I got it, and the Executors are driving it on as fast as they can, in Hopes to get a Hearing by Michaelmas Term ; and in order to that we shall be examining the Proofs of our Witnesses, which are a great many and very strong, and will demonstrate to yᵉ Court yᵗ he is forsworn in his whole Answer, excepting one false Article, which he owns to have been wrong, and wh. amounts to but £60, wh. he acknowledges he recᵈ of yᵉ Duke of *Newcastle* and did not bring into his Acctˢ. You will remember yᵉ Conversation wʰ. I had with you concerning the Mortgage of the Interest of it, wʰ. you told me you had paid in 1711 to Mr. *Guidott,* wʰ. you certainly did pay to him ; and it appears by several Acctˢ and Memorandums to be so. But Mr. *Guidott* did not put it into the Duke of *Marlborough's* Acctˢ wh. he passd in 1712 in a great Hurry, wⁿ. the Duke of *Marlborough* was going out of *England*; but if he had had ever so much Time to look into Acct[s], it was hardly possible for him to remember all the Mortgages or Interests y[t] Mr. *Guidott* has rec[d].; and I am told by y[e] most able Counsel in *England* y[t] tho you can't unravel an Acc[t] sign'd many Years ago, yet the Discharge of the Acc[t] can go no further than of y[e] Sums y[t] are in it. The Executors don't dispute w[t] the Duke of *Marlborough* has given his Hand for, but there is a great deal besides yours which Mr. *Guidott* has rec[d]. and never brought into his Acc[t], all which will appear very plain. I am sorry to interrupt y[e] Pleasure w[h] I am sure you have in Building, but as it is absolutely necessary to examine you upon the Interrogatories drawn for this Cause, I desire to know when it will be most convenient for you to be in Town, or whether you would like better to have a Commission sent to you into the Country to save you the Trouble. I don't write to dear Mrs. *Jennens*, because I know she hates writing, but I can't help asking her by you to send me in Writing exactly what she advis'd should be done to *Dye's* Neck, for I would be very exact in the Matter, and I am not sure y[t] I remember all y[t] she told me. I have seen a very reasonable Woman since she was in Town who would fain have done Something to her Neck, but as my Lady *Masham* had a Child dyd with Remedies of y[t] sort, I must not do any Thing with[t] the Advice of a Physician, who thought it better to do Nothing, and I am apt to hope y[t] in some Time *Dye's* Neck will be well, since her Sister *Bateman*

had y.ᵉ same Swelling and has not the least now.
However, I would try any Thing so innocent as
Mrs. *Jennings* propos'd, because that can do no
Hurt. I should be glad to send you w.ᵗ Venison
you car'd for, but I have been enquiring how far you
are from either of my Parks, and I think it is im-
practicable. But I can give Warrants to some of the
Duke of *Grafton*'s Friends, whose Forest I am told is
convenient, to serve you in Exchange for Venison for
you. But in y.ᵉ mean Time I send you a Warrant upon
Woodstock Park for your Brother, where it us'd to
be carry'd very easyly, and I hope he likes it as well as
he us'd to do. And if you have any other Friends
y.ᵗ you would have Venison for that lie convenient for
Woodstock or for *Windsor*, pray make no Difficulty
in letting me know what you would have order'd,
for I have a great deal of Venison in my Power, and
wish I had any Thing of more Consequence y.ᵗ was
in the least agreeable to you, to whom I shall ever be
A most faithful humble Servant,

S. MARLBOROUGH.

I know People in the Country like News, and I
am very sorry y.ᵗ I can't entertain you with it, the
Town being very dull and empty.

This Leter is write by my new Secretary, the
Duke of *Bedford*, which you will read with more
Ease than my rediculous Hand. Hee has come to
Town about his own Businesse, and he has turn'd
Dye out of her Place of my Secretary, which you
know is a common Thing in this Age for Ministers

to trip up one another's Heels. He is the best Servant and Minister that ever I had, and hee is so far from being lazy that he copys out all my Papers that I have. Hee is certainly a perfect Miracle of his Age. I think Providence designs to make me amends for some of my past Sufferings by the Goodnesse and Kindnesse of this young Man, for I am told by severall of my Friends that hee says hee loves me of all Things; and I am sure that I will preserve it by doing every Thing that I can to serve him.

No. 29.

To Mr. Jennens.

July ye 24th, 1725, *London.*

I give you many Thanks for the Favour of yours of the 10th *July*. I did not receive it of the right Post Day, but a Day later; but I writ imediately to Mr. *Waller* concerning what you desird about the Interrogatories, and I enclose his Answer to it, which I suppose will inform you more perfectly than any Thing I can say, who have never studied that Business till I was forc'd to it by the many Frauds; but however, I imagine that your Interrogatories will be to the following Purposes: whether you did not tell me in the Presence of *Charles Hodges,* upon my showing you a State of the Debts upon Sir *William Gostwick's* Estate, that you had paid off the £2,500, with the Interest due upon it, to Mr. *Guidott* in 1711. It is writ in Mr. *Guidott's* Book of Mortgages, in his Clerk's Hand, to the same Effect, and perhaps you may be asked whether you paid it in Mony or Bills, and to what Goldsmith, for the Duke of *Marlborough's* Use. But I don't know whether that will be an Interrogatory, tho I do know that the Duke of *Marlborough* never receivd any of his Mortgages himself, tho Nobody would pay their Money without his Hand to their Discharges; and Mr. *Guidott* has brought into his Accounts the Money received upon Mortgages except yours and the £3,000 of the Dutchess of *Bedford*. Yours should have been brought in the Accounts signed when he was in so much Trouble going out of *England*, and I suppose that tempted Mr. *Guidott* to omitt it, thinking it would never be discovered; but all his Frauds will be proved very plainly that I have found out; and the best Counsel in *England* tells me that my Lord *Marlborough's* setting his Hand to Mr. *Guidott's* Accounts does not discharge him of any Sums but what are in those Accounts. I remember when I first spoke to you upon this Matter you told me the whole Story, how Mr. *Guidott* had desir'd my Lord *Marlborough* to take your Mortgage upon S^r. W^m. *Gostwick's* Estate, which was Part of your Wife's Portion, and to continue a Mortgage of £2,500 upon Mr. *Daniel's* Estate till it was easy to you to pay it; and you added that you were very sorry that you were the unlucky Occation of beginning the Mortgage upon S^r. W^m. *Gostwick*, which would occation so much Loss. You will see by Mr. *Waller's* Letter that the Time is not fix'd for the Interrogatories. If they happen whilst I am in Town, it will be only the Trouble of a Journey, which will do you Good, and you may be at your own House with few Servants, and be so good as to dine with me whilst you like to stay here. I give you and dear Mrs. *Jennens* a great many Thanks for all your kind Expressions to me ; and tho you are pleased to be very merry upon giving up your own Judgment to follow a Ladies' Fancy, I am satisfied that Nobody will ever suffer by taking Mrs. *Jennens's* Advice. *Dye* returns her Thanks with me, and is very grateful for what you say concerning her, for you will allways command what Venison you please out of my Parks in the Season that seems most acceptable to you. What you say of the Duke of *Bedford* is certainly true, and I hope he and some other young Ones that I know will in Time take care of our Property, if it be'nt gone before they have the Power to do it. My humble Service to dear Mrs. *Jennens*, which is all that I will trouble you with at this Time, but the Assurance of being

Your most faithfull

And most obedient Servant,

S. MARLBOROUGH.

[*Mr. Robert Jennins to the Duchess of Marlborough.*

Madam,—By *Waller's* to your Grace I find my Examination is to be in Person ; and since it must be so, let my Sufferings in the Work be what it will, if Mr. *Waller* is sure the Hearing can be brought on by *Michaelmas Term*, which knowing the Dilatorinesse of *Chancery* I doubt, will have my Interrogatories ready, and give me some few Days Notice, I certainly will attend in *London*. The Conversation your Grace is pleased to remember with me about my Mortgage to the Duke of *Marlborough* before Mr. Charles *Hodges* is, in the main, very right; but exactly the Expression then of paying the Money to Mr. *Guidott* I cannot swear to; but when you told me there would be a Dispute between the *Executors* and Mr. *Guidott* for that Money, I did or would have explained it to you. I am sure I paid the Principal and Interest to a Farthing in a Bank and a Goldsmith's Note, I believe Sir Robert *Child's* and *Company;* and when I paid them to the Duke he bid my Cousin *Guidott* look upon them and see that they were right. I gave them to him, and he told his Grace they were so. Then he signed the Receipt upon the Back of the Deed, and I think it is witnessed by two of his Servants. I took my Deed, went away, and left them togeather; but when Peeple that have had Transactions fall into Dispute that have made a Noise in the World, I think a Justiciary Explanation the best Way to shew how every Party has behaved in the Dispute; that the Folly or Knavery may be laid upon the right Person. I give you many Thanks for your kind Invitation, being

Your Grace's

Most obedient

humble Servant,

ROBERT JENNINS.

Acton, 27th *July,* 1725.

The Duchess of *Marlborough's* answer to this Letter was as follows] :—

To Mr. *Jennins.*

No. 30.

August 7, 1725, *London.*

Being desirous to trouble you as little as possible, I write this to let you know that I find it will not be necessary for you to come to *London* sooner than, I believe, your own Businesse may require you to be, for I was with the Counsel last Night till one o'Clock; and they say that there must be a Plea set down to be argued before the Wittnesse can be examined, unless any of them should be in Danger of dying, which I hope is not your Case. This will delay this Cause some Time longer. I am not yet Lawyer enough to be sure that I express this right, but I believe what I write will be sufficient for you to guess at my Meaning, and I hope you will forgive me for saying that I dont quite understand your Letter of the 27th of *July* You say that what I write to you of our Conversation concerning your paying the Mony lent you by the Duke of *Marlborough* to Mr. *Guidott* is, in the main, very right. You add that you believe your Note was upon Sir R. *Child,* which it most certainly was, for you must know that Mr. *Guidott* derected all the Money received upon the Duke of *Marlborough's* Account to him, who was his Brother in Law; and there can be no Doubt that he had a great Share of the Produce of it; for Mr. *Guidott,* as it appears in his Accounts, kept vast Ballance in his Hands, that he ought to have paid to Mr. *Edwards* for Improvement; but there is no Remedy for such Losses. You say that you gave your Notes to your Cousin *Guidott*, as the Duke bid you, to see if they were right, and that he said they were so; then the Duke of *Marlborough* signed, and you took your Deed and went away: this shews that Mr. *Guidott* had the Notes from you, and the Duke of *Marlborough's* saying he should count them shews that he was to have them; for if the Duke of *Marlborough* had been to keep the Notes, he would have counted them himself. But through the whole Accounts, tho he was to sign the Mortgages, Mr. *Guidott* received the Money, and has brought them all to Account, except yours and the Dutchesse of *Bedford's*, which is so plain a Case that I need say Nothing of that; for Mr. *Guidott*, in Effect, has been forced to own that, but he has shewn at the same Time that he was very desirous to have sunk that, as well as he has done many Sums for Interest paid to him, and your Mortgage, and the Interest of one Year paid in 1711 is just the same Thing as the Dutchess of *Bedford's*; and it is enterd in Mr. Charles *Widmore* Hand, in the Book of Mortgages, 16 *Feb.*, 1711—Received of Mr. *Jennins* 2625-9- in full, for Principal and Interest, but no where charged in Mr. *Guidott's* Accounts. The poor Duke of *Marlborough* going out of *England* just as the Accounts were signed on the 20th *November*, 1712, was, to be sure, one Temptation to leave out that Sum and some others for Interest, for he knew at

that Time it would never be examined into, and
indeed he had seen so much of the Duke of *Marlborough's* Reliance upon him that he might very
safely have done the same Thing at any other Time;
for you know that he was always very carless as
to the examining his Accounts. As to your Answer
upon the Interrogatories, you know that I asked you
twice over if you had not paid your Mortgage to
Mr. *Guidott* in 1711, and you answer'd both Times,
Yes, in the Presence of Mr. *Hodges*, and this I take
to be the same Thing as if you had said in direct
Words that you had paid the Sum wanting—your
self—to Mr. *Guidott*. Since when I asked that
Question, you answer'd Yes, and *Hodges* writ it
down that he might be sure to make no Mistake in
his Evidence, when he was call'd upon to satisfy
what you and I had said. You say that you did or
would have explained Something of this Matter.
Would or did is very different, and I have asked
Hodges what pas'd more than he writ, and he said
Nothing. I am sure I could refuse Nothing that you
had a Mind to say to me upon any Subject; and in
that Conversation you mention, when I asked who
you paid the Mortgage to, I did not say any Thing of
the Executors' disire of calling Mr. *Guidott* to an
Account for the Money he had received, and not
charged; but let this be as it will, it signifies
Nothing, for it is a very short and plain Question—
Wether I did not ask you before *Hodges* if you had
paid the Money to Mr. *Guidott*, and you answerd
Yes, twice over; and if I had not this Proof, the

Account Book shews it so plainly that the Executors can't fail of having Justice done them, which is all that I ever can disire upon any Subject what so ever. My humble Service to dear Mrs. *Jennins*. I hope in *October* to see you both very well at *London*, and that you will be well pleased with your Building. I am sure I should be so if I could see it,

Who am your most

Faithful humble Servant,

S. MARLBOROUGH.

To this Letter Mr. *Jennens* wrote the following reply :—

Madam,—I am much obliged to your Grace for preventing my coming to *London* before it was necessary, for I had order'd Horses to meet me on the Road on *Sunday*, that I might have made my Journey in one Day. I was in Hopes that the more strictly you had examined into my Cousin *Guidott's* Conduct, the more innocent he would have appeared in your Thoughts, for I always took him for a sincere honest Man ; but since it proves the contrary, and as my Transactions with him on the Duke's Account form the blackest Accusation, I beg that my Interrogatories may be as strict and full as possible, that what I have done may be shewn as it is done. If your Grace and Mr. *Hodges* both agree in the Expression of my paying the Money to Mr. *Guidott*, to be sure it was so—what I meant by explaining to you was that he took the

Bills from me, by the Duke's Order, to see if they were right, which I think makes it much the same Thing.

    I am
      Your Grace's most
        Devoted humble Searvant,
          ROBERT JENNENS.

Acton, 12 *August,* 1725.]

[*To the foregoing Correspondence there is appended the following, but not in the Duchess's handwriting :*—

Notwithstanding these shuffling Letters of Mr. *Jennens,* he was examined, and his Evidence is in the Case. Most People know his Character. But as he had a Mind to appear a Man of Honour, and I knew that Mr. *Hodges* would swear what he had said before him, which he had unfortunately told the Dutchess before he knew there would be a Law Suit, what more could he do in this Case, to return the Services of Mr. *Guidott,* who had eased him of so bad a Mortgage, then to give his Evidence as he did—that he had given the Bills to Mr. *Guidott* to count, and that when his Mortgage was discharg'd he took his Deed and left them together? Mr. *Jennens* had another Veiw besides what I have mention'd of Gratitude : he hoped that his Son might be Mr. *Guidott's* Heir, and therefore it was natural in him to assist Mr. *Guidott* as far as it consisted with his high Points of Honour.]

No. 31.

To Mrs. *Jennens*.

Thursday, past ten in the morning.

This is to tell my dear Mrs. *Jenyns* that 'tis so cold that I dare not goe out this Morning, but I hope you and Mr. *Jenyns* will do me the Favour to dine with me at Half an Hour past Three, whos Company is allways very agreeable to me.

Percivall Heart, of Sorte's *Coffee-house*, is the Name of the Witnesse, and what he swears was concerning a Conversation at Mr. *Guidott's*, and in the Company of Marmaduke *Allington*. When Mr. *Jenyns* comes he shall read what he says : in the mean Time I think it amounts to Nothing but to show that whatever good Mr. *Jenyns* wishd to do him he would put a Slur upon if he could.

[*The following are appended to the above in the MS. Collection of Letters :—*

Grandmama is in so great a Hurry with having the Interrogatoris settled by the Council at which she is present in order to expose all the foul Proceedings of Mr. *Guidott*, that she begs your Pardon that she can't write to you her self ; but as you desired to know about what Time they will be ready for you, she orders me to lett you know that Mr. *Waller* thinks that they will be ready in ten Days, or soon after, and that you may be examined imediately after they are settled. I can't end this without assuring dear Mrs. *Jennens* and you that I am your most

Obedient humble Servant,

D. SPENCER.

July 31, 1725.

I cant in Hon^r. omit immediately returning Thanks to assuire Lady *Spencer* for the Favour of a Letter, an old Man being seldom us'd to such fine Things, and at the same Time beg your Lady^shp. to interceed with Mr. *Waller* that he would give me a Week's Notice when he is sure the Interogatories are held. With our humble Duties to Lady Dutchess, and as soon as we come to *London* will pay our Duties to her, and personally return our Thankes to your Ladyship, being

Y^r most obedient,

Humble Servant,

R. A. JENNENS.]

No. 32.

To Mrs. Jennens.

Aug. 21, 1725, *London.*

My good Secretary not being up, you must be contented this Time to be troubled with my own rediculous Hand, for I have a Mind to thank you before I goe to *Windsor* for the Favour of yours of the 12th of this Month, tho I am not sure that I have not don it allready, for I live in such a perpetuall Hurry of Businesse and Labour from Morning to Night, like a Pack-horse, and I think my Head is

sometimes a little turnd; and as I have often designd to write to you, I am not certain whether I
have don it or not; but if this happens to be a Repetition, I hope you will forgive me. There is no
possibility of giving you any Trouble in Mr. *Guidott's* Affair sooner than the Middle of *October*: how
much longer it will bee I don't know, but I will
write to you again when 'tis necessary to trouble
you about it. I have spent many Days in trying to
prevent great Abuses and Losses to the Estate and
to very good Effect, and I think myself oblidged to do
all I can for the Duke of *Marlborough's* Posterity,
whoever enjoys his Forest Estate. I believe I have
not given you an Account of one Thing that has
been discovered lately in looking over Acquittances
which have been brought me by an Agent to the
late Duchess of *Bedford*. I have seen six Acquittances for Interest Mony, all signd by *Will. Guidott;*
and before he putt his Name he writes in his own
Hand, receiv'd by the Duke of *Marlborough's* Direc-
tion and for his Use. The last of those Acquittances
is for Interest where hee received the Principall,
which he never so much as mentions in his Accounts,
and forswore it for a long Time. I don't no whether
hee is come to own that Sum yet, but it is but for
one Year's Interest when the Principall Mony was
paid in, which he likewise would fain have sunk.
Such a Summ as that would not have been worth
the Trouble of taking Notice of; but as the Whole is
very considerable, every Thing must be brought to
Light in such a Cause; and he has thrown so much

Dust at me, that for my own Honour, as well as for
the Interest of my Family, I must expose him; and
'tis certain hee will make a worse Figure when all
comes out than ever was before seen in *Westminster
Hall.* There are at least two five hundred Pounds
sunk of the Duke of *Bedford's* Interest, for which
hee got the Duke of *Marlborough's* Hand, but one
of them is write in Mr. *Guidott's* own Hand; and
there being such a Number of Acquittances signed by
Mr. *Guidott* for that Mortgage shews that they had
no Scruple in paying for Mr. *Guidott's* Discharge,
which makes me think that he was so ingenious as
to get the Duke of *Marlborough* to sign some Times,
thinking that Way might help him better to sink
such Mony; but what I have mentiond before sunk
was in *Feb.* 1716, signd by Mr. *Guidott*, and not
brought to Account. I suppose the Duke of *Marlborough's* being sick tempted him to do that, and I
don't find a Mistake of one Shilling in all the
Accounts of so many Yeares, to the Prejudice of
Mr. *Guidott*, and if they had not been designd for
more, would never have been so constant as to make
all the Occasions fall upon the Duke of *Marlborough.*

I am glad you will bee able to cover your Hous
this Season, when I fancy it will bee dry, because
we have had yet but a very few Days of Summer.
When I leave *Windsor*, which will bee the first
Week in *Sep.*, I shall goe for ten Days or a Fortnight to *Blenheim*, where I shall allmost fill the At-
tuick Story with Friends; but not one that will ever
be so agreeable as dear Mrs. *Jennens* will ever be

to me. I have had a Letter lately from a very good Judge who says he has been at *Blenheim*, and that the Lake Cascade Slopes above the Bridge are all finish'd and as beautifull as can bee imagin'd, the Banks being coverd with a most delightful Verdure; the Canals are allso finish'd the whole Length of the Medow under the Wood, and there are a hundred Men at Work sloping the Hill near *Rosamond's* Well; and when all the Banks are don in the same Manner, and the whole Design compleat'd, it will certainly bee a wonderfull fine Place, and I believe will be liked by every Body, and I am glad it will bee so, because it was the dear Duke of *Marlborough's* Passion to have it don; but in 1716 it was so terrible an Undertaking that I am sure I should never have ventur'd upon it if you had not push'd me on to do it. I wish you better Luck in your Undertakings, which I am sure will bee rightly orderd in all Respects, and a much more agreeable and comfortable Place to live in all the Year round, with a few good Friends, than ever *Blenheim* will bee, that has and will cost so vast a Sum. I long to see it, and hope to doe it before I dye, when I am so hapy as to have less to do then I have at present. My sincere, humble Services to Mrs. *Jennens*, which shall conclude this tedious Leter from your most faithfull humble Servant.

S. MARLBOROUGH.

No. 33.

To Mr. Jennens.

October 20, 1725.

My Secretary *Di* is not up: however, I will not give you the Trouble of reading a Letter in my ugly Hand, which is to acquaint you that I came to *London* about Mr. *Guidott's* Cause, which was only a Thing of Form concerning the arguing of the Plea; you know there is very little of the Merits of the Cause that appears at first; however, I remark'd that my *Lord Chancellor* took particular Care to explain himself to Mr. *Guidott's* Counsell, that he would not bar the Executors from looking back into Accounts where there was Cause for it; and he said in the Court that he made no Difference between Accounts with or without, Errors excepted, wherever there did appear Errors; and that is all that the Executors, or even I, shall ever desire, and these Errors will be so strongly made out, both from Mr. *Guidott's* own Accounts, as well as the Evidences, that I can't apprehend there is the least Doubt of Success in what is so demonstrably plain and just, so that I hope this Suit will soon come to a Conclusion, for every Body says my *Lord Chancellor* makes great Dispatch in every Thing. The Reason of my giving you this Trouble, is to know when your own Occasions will make it agreeable to you to come to *London*, wishing that you may have no Sort of Uneasiness on my Account. I have this Day begun to examine some of the Witnesses, and shall go on to

examine them all as fast as I can, that Publication
may be made for the hearing in a proper Time. I
hope you are in good Health and dear Mrs. *Jennens*,
who am, with great Truth, her and your

Faithfull humble Servant,

S. MARLBOROUGH.

No. 34.

To Mr. Jennens.

London, Octr. 26, 1725.

I have received the Favour of your Letter dated
the 23rd of this Month, by which I imagine that it
will be more convenient to you to deferr as long
as I can your Examination, which must be about
the 20th of *Nov*ʳ· ; but I will examin as many other
Witnesses as I can before I send to you, and then I
will be sure to give you 4 or 5 Days Notice before
the Time, and will answer that you shall not come
till the Examiner is ready to receive your Evidence,
that it may be dispatched as soon as 'tis possible ;
and if my takeing more Trouble than I do could ease
you of any Thing, I should be extream glad of it.
I am very sorry that every Thing in your House is
not dispatchd to your Mind, but you say half the
Roofe is cover'd, and I hope it may be quite secur'd
before any ill Weather comes ; and if it should not be
all done, I hope it will not be prejudiciall, because I
know that *Blenheim* Works were stopd in 1714, and
some Part of the Gallery was uncover'd till 1717.
But let what will happen as to the covering your
House, I am sure in the End it will be a reasonable

and an agreeable Building, and upon my Word I
take a Pleasure in that Thought for your sake, and
dear Mrs. *Jennens's*, who I hope will come to *London*
with you, though your Stay be ever so short, that she
may take Care of you as she has done for so many
Years, and at the same Time give me the Satisfaction of seeing her who am faithfully hers and your

Most obedient

Humble Servant,

S. MARLBOROUGH.

Dye presents her humble Dutty to her dear
Mother.

No. 35.

To Mr. Jennens.

Nov. 2, 1725.

In my last I writ you Word that about the 20th
of this Month would be Time enough for your coming to Town, but as I find you intend to go back
again as soon as you have answered the Interrogatory, perhaps it may be as convenient to you to
come sooner, and it w^d be much better for me,
because I want to go out of Town, and I can't go
till I have finish'd my Part in so material a Business. All the Witnesses that are of the greatest
Consequence are examined, and if you will please to
let me know the soonest Day that you will be in
Town I will take Care that you shall not be detain'd
one Hour longer than you like to stay, and I

suppose your Evidence will not take a Quarter of an Hour with the Examiner.

I have the Satisfaction to see already that the Executors' Cause will be very strong, and the Charges proved plainly upon Mr. *Guidott;* and whatever the Event of some inconsiderable Particulars may be at Law, yet I shall be able to demonstrate that I am in the Right of every Thing in that Affair, which I like better than Mony.

Pray present my humble Service to dear Mrs. *Jennens*, and believe me

Your most faithfull
And most humble Servant,
S. MARLBOROUGH.

I make no Excuses for making Use of another Hand, because it will be easier for you to read, and my Head aches a little.

No. 36.

To Mr. Jennens.

Nov. 6th, 1725.

I think I omitted in my last Letter to let you know that it will be necessary to produce the Deed of Mortgage cancelled, and the Acquittances for the Interest, which I think are not likely to be in the Country : however, it is carefull in me, you will allow, to put you in Mind of them.   I was in Hope of having an Answer to my Letter from you last Post. I hear Mr. *Guidott* has been so politick as to make it be put into the Prints that he had got the better in his Cause ; 'tis very far from that, but if he pleases himself with it, it does the Ex^rs. no hurt no more than the Prints do when they marry People.   I hope I shall hear soon when you'll be in Town, to prepare Things for you that you may not stay.   My humble Service to dear Mrs. *Jennens*, who am your most faithfull and most humble Servant,

S. MARLBOROUGH.

Dye presents her humble Dutty to her dear Mother.

No. 37.

To Mr. Jennens.

London, Nov. 8, 1725.

I am extream sorry that the Weather has been so bad for your Journey, for tho I am much concerned to do Justice to the Duke of *Marlborough's* Family, it would be a great Trouble to me if your Health sh^d suffer upon that Account.   Mr. *Waller* sends me Word that the Examiner has promised to examine you as soon as you come, and it may be done if you please Tonight; and if after that is over you are not too weary to like to have a Party at *Embro*, I shall have one at my House that won't be disagreeable to you, who am

Your most faithfull
Humble Servant,
S. MARLBOROUGH.

[*Here an important hiatus in this correspondence occurs, evidently occasioned by the death of Mr. Robert Jennins, to whom most of the Letters are addressed. The only remaining letter in the collection is the following to his widow*] :—

No. 38.

To Mrs. Jennens.

Feb. 28, 172$\frac{5}{6}$.

I am so lame of one of my Feet, by having strain'd it by going up so many Steps, that I can't come to you Today, dear Mrs. *Jennens*, as I wish'd to have done. But when I came Home last Night, I found two very knowing Men at my House, and having heard by Accident that poor Mr. *Jennens* died without a Will, I could not forbear asking these Lords, for my own Satisfaction, remembering very well that your Settlement, whatever it was, must have been so long ago, at your Marriage, when there could not be a tolerable Provision made for you. They told me that whatever you had accepted of then in Land for your Jointure twas probable, as Writings are generally made, would debar you from any greater Share of Land Estate which Mr. *Jennens* might have ; but that whatever personal Estate he had, which all Stocks are reckon'd by the Law, you would certainly have a Third Part of that in your own Power to dispose of ; and if Mr. *Jennens* was a Freeman of the *City*, as I think I have heard he was, in that Case your Proportion will be greater ; for the City Law is, that if a Man dies without a

Will, the Wife has One Third Part of the Whole,
the Children have another Third Part, and the
Husband's Third Part, which he might have dispos'd
of by a Will; he not having made one, the Wife
will have a Third Part of that Third Part; and
some People are of Opinion, that when there is but
one Child the Wife will have Half; but my Authority
for this is not so well grounded as for all the rest.
I have had a very good Lawyer's Opinion this
Morning upon this Matter, who confirms to me all
that I have writ but the last, and in that he is a
little doubtfull. I was ask'd Abundance of Questions
which I would say Nothing to, but as follows, that
it was not a Time to speak to you upon any Thing
of this Matter, and that what I said was from my
own Memory of Things that I knew long ago. But
I remember that Part of your Portion was the
Mortgage upon *Gostwick's Estate*, but I knew Nothing
how that was settl'd. But I see plainly by what
these learned People have told me, the worst Thing
that can happen to you in this Affair is, that if you
have a Jointure settl'd upon you in Marriage in
Land, you can then have no more out of Land then
what is settl'd; but out of all other Effects it will be
as I have already told you. Let me hear how you
do by Word of Mouth. I expect no Answer to
these Particulars, who am for ever your most affectionate humble Servant,

S. MARLBOROUGH.

I am thoroughly persuaded in my own Mind, that poor Mr. *Jennens*, that lov'd you so well, and must be sensible of your Merit, would not have died without making his Will, but that he knew the Law, and knew that you would be provided for according to his own Intention, whenever that dismal Day happened.